This is a wonderfully lu[...] neglected doctrine. It wil[...] confidence in the Bible [...] sovereign, speaking God.

Vaughan Roberts
Rector of St Ebbe's, Oxford
Director of Proclamation Trust
Author of several books, including *God's Big Picture* and
Battle's Christians Face

We who live after the history of special revelation that preceded the Bible and led to its canonical form rightly assume that God has preserved that revelation for us in the Bible we possess today. But not many Christians reflect on this assumption, and even fewer know how to defend it. In this slim but potent book, Richard Brash not only urges us to 'mind the gap' in our thinking on Scripture's preservation through the ages, he shows us how to close this gap by looking to the teaching of Scripture itself. This book, written by a true pastor-scholar, will make you marvel at the wisdom, power, and love of God, whose written Word, like Himself, is everlastingly sure.

R. Carlton Wynne
Assistant Professor, Systematic Theology and Apologetics,
Westminster Theological Seminary, Glenside, Pennsylvania

A CHRISTIAN'S POCKET GUIDE TO

HOW GOD PRESERVED
THE BIBLE

RICHARD BRASH

CHRISTIAN
FOCUS

Scripture quotations are from *The Holy Bible, English Standard Version*, copyright © 2001 by Crossway Bibles, a publishing ministry of Good News Publishers. Used by permission. All rights reserved. ESV Text Edition: 2011.

Copyright © Richard Brash 2019

paperback ISBN 978-1-5271-0421-1
epub ISBN 978-1-5271-0482-2
mobi ISBN 978-1-5271-0483-9

10 9 8 7 6 5 4 3 2 1

Published in 2019 by
Christian Focus Publications Ltd,
Geanies House, Fearn, Ross-shire,
IV20 1TW, Scotland, Great Britain
www.christianfocus.com

Cover design by Daniel Van Straaten

Printed by Norhaven

CONTENTS

⚠ Warning
🖉 Don't Forget
⑦ Stop and Think
🌟 Point of Interest

PREFACE

This book is about the providential preservation of Scripture. I first became interested in this subject when serving as an associate minister at St Ebbe's Church in Oxford, where some (very bright!) graduate students began asking me questions about 'how we got the Bible.' In seminary, I had learned how to explain the inspiration of Scripture. I'd also been taught about the issues of canon-formation and text-criticism. These things were helpful, up to a point. But I began to realise that, for some students at least, there were deeper questions in the background. These were questions about what *God* was doing in the preservation of Scripture, and they seemed to demand a more 'theological' response, grounded in the doctrines of God and his outer works (his works in relation to creation), particularly that of providence.

These questions led me into graduate work in systematic and historical theology, particularly on the development of the Reformed doctrine of the providential preservation of Scripture. All the time, I was thinking about how to communicate the key ideas to the students I ministered to in Oxford, either to strengthen their trust in God and his Word, or to persuade them to begin trusting for the first time. This book is largely the fruit of that work.

In many ways, then, this book complements other books about 'how we got the Bible,' such as the excellent volume by Gregory Lanier in this series. Its focus is different, however, in that the approach is primarily *doctrinal*. The providential preservation of Scripture is a relatively neglected doctrine, not so much because it is denied or ignored, but mostly because it is presumed rather than thought through or defended.[1] It's my hope that this book will contribute to both our doctrinal thinking and our apologetics.

I'm deeply grateful to Dr Elijah Hixson, who took the time to read and comment on the manuscript, saving me from a number of mistakes relating to New Testament textual criticism, among other things. Any remaining errors are mine.

Reformed reflections on the providence of God frequently invoke the category of 'mystery.' For my wife Yuko and me, having sensed our primary calling as missionaries to the Japanese, a move from Tokyo to Oxford seemed at first like something of a 'mysterious' detour. In God's providence, our five years in Oxford were happy and blessed ones, and—we trust—will turn out to have been useful in forming us for future ministry in Japan. Serving the students of *Thesis* at St Ebbe's was the main context for our work in those years: this book is dedicated, with affection, to them.

Note: In this book, I refer to the 'Word' of God (capitalised), whether the reference is to the Second Person of the Trinity (as in John 1:1), or to the spoken or written Word of God, except when I am quoting other published works that do not capitalise 'Word.' Sometimes, I leave the referent intentionally ambiguous, so that both the Second Person of the Trinity *and* the written Word are included. However, 'words' of God in the plural is not capitalised.

INTRODUCTION: MIND THE GAP

I remember a friend at university complaining to me, 'We get lots of teaching at church about being single. And lots of teaching about being married. What I want is some teaching about how you get from one state to the other.' What my friend had identified was indeed a significant gap. (He is now happily married!)

A similar 'gap' often opens up in what we believe—or teach—about the Bible. We might be able to talk about what God did in the past, in the process of the Bible being written down (that's called inspiration). And we may also be able to give an account of what God does today, in taking the words in our Bibles and applying them to our hearts so that we understand the message and respond (that's called illumination). These are both divine works usually ascribed in particular to the Holy Spirit. Many Christians are familiar with them to some degree. But we don't often have much to say about what

God is, or was, doing in the centuries-long process of getting the inspired words of Scripture on to a page (or smart-phone screen) that we can read today.

What does the Holy Spirit do in respect of the Bible—if indeed he does anything at all—between his works of inspiration and illumination? This book has been written to help fill in the gap. It's written with two particular groups of people in mind. First, it's a book for Christians who would like to have greater confidence that the Bible they read is 'accurate.' Second, it's a book for non-Christians or those looking into Christian faith who might have doubts or questions at precisely this point. This second group of people may well include atheists, or agnostics, or even Muslims, for reasons that will become clear.

Because there are lots of great books available about the trustworthiness of Scripture, I need to spend some time in this introduction making clear exactly what I'm setting out to do in this book. Hopefully that will explain why this particular book is important, and different from other books. I'll also try to make clear what I'm *not* aiming to do—usually because it's been done elsewhere—so that you as a reader have the right expectations for what lies ahead.

When I talk about the Bible being 'accurate,' I don't mean 'accurate' in the usual sense of that word, as 'true' or 'free from error.'[2] In this book, I'm going to take it as a given that what the biblical writers first wrote was 'inspired' by the Holy Spirit of God, and therefore was—and is—true and free from error in everything it affirms.

What the prophets and apostles wrote when they first 'inscripturated' the books of the Bible was made up of normal words in normal human languages (Hebrew, Aramaic and Greek) reflecting their own individual styles, personalities and circumstances. On some special occasions, there was—strictly speaking—no human author of the original words of Scripture. According to Exodus 31:18, Moses was given the decalogue (or the Ten Commandments) by God himself, on 'two tablets of the testimony, tablets of stone, written with the finger of God.' This was an exceptional occurrence: most of the time, the words of the Bible were written down by human authors. But at the same time, God was at work to ensure that all the words of the biblical writers were also his words, breathed out by his Spirit. This is called the doctrine of inspiration. One of its implications is that, as the Word of God written, the Bible contains no errors in what it asserts. This is called the doctrine of inerrancy.

Of course, to say that the Bible is inspired and inerrant is to make some big claims. I'm not avoiding these issues, but they are not the main subject of this book, and they have been well articulated and defended elsewhere. If you'd like to think more about inspiration or inerrancy, you may want to start with some of the general books on the doctrine of Scripture in the 'suggestions for further reading' section at the end of this book.

The etymology of our English word 'accurate' (from the Latin *accuratus* = 'taken care of, having been taken care of') points to a different concern, which is the focus of this book. That is, how can I account for the claim that the Bible I read *today* is the Word of God? Can I have confidence that this is the case?

You might never have considered these questions. After all, lots of things in life we take on trust. We believe that the bus timetable will be accurate, more or less, without thinking too much about who actually typed it up or where it was printed, let alone whether anyone was overseeing the process, 'taking care' of the text. In the Christian life, we have even more reason to take such things on trust, because we trust in God. When we believe in Jesus, we take the Bible to be God's Word—trustworthy and true—even though we can't understand it all, and probably haven't read it all either. In all likelihood you have no idea who typed up the text of your Bible, or where it was printed, or who made what decisions about what particular words to use.

Even so, if you're a Christian, I expect you often have the sheep-like experience of listening to the voice of the Shepherd speak to you when the Bible is read and preached. (See John chapter 10 for the Shepherd/sheep analogy.) In other words, at some deep, 'spiritual' level, you just *know* that the Bible you're hearing is God's Word. That's a good Christian instinct, and I don't intend to discourage it at all.

But if we stop to think about it (which we should) there are a number of steps that we have assumed when we apply this instinct. Two of these steps are particularly important. First, and perhaps most obviously, the Bible you read is probably *not* written in Hebrew, Aramaic or Greek. You're probably aware of the existence of many different Bible translations. The different translations aren't just about style—sometimes they mean different things. Is one translation more 'accurate' than another? How can we tell? Second, we don't have any of the original manuscripts of the Bible. The actual leather on which a book like *Genesis* was originally written (or the papyrus on which a letter like *First Corinthians* was originally written) is simply not available to us.[3] These originals are known as the *autographs*, and they almost certainly don't exist any more. What we *do* have (in various museums and libraries around the world) is a collection of manuscripts (hand-written documents) of varying age and quality that are *copies* of copies of the autographs. The majority are probably copies of copies of copies... and so on. And, as far as I know, without exception, no two of these manuscripts are exactly the same. So, which manuscript is 'accurate'? Where exactly *is* God's Word? Might bits of it have been lost? Or added in? How can we tell?

These two issues are obviously of great practical importance. Even if God inspired the text of, say, *Galatians* (which he did!) that is of limited benefit to us if we follow a badly-copied Greek manuscript of *Galatians*, full of mistakes. The problem is compounded when we, or someone else, mis-translates that bad manuscript into bad English, and then an editor fails to pick up on the errors. We could end up with all kinds of problems.

In 1631, the (in)famous 'Wicked Bible' was published in London. The typesetters made a mistake in the text of

The original manuscripts of the Bible books are known as the autographs. In distinction from the autographs, copies or transcripts that still exist today are called apographs. It's extremely unlikely that there are any 'direct' copies of the biblical autographs available to us. Almost all the apographs we now have are probably the result of a long and complex process of copying copies.

Exodus 20:14, omitting the word 'not,' so that the sixth commandment read, 'Thou shalt commit adultery.' The publishers were fined £300 and deprived of their printing licence. That is, of course, a silly (but true) example of how texts can be changed, in this case inadvertently. In this particular instance, the problem was readily noticed and rectified, and hopefully no great damage was done. (All existing copies of the 'Wicked Bible' were ordered to be burned, although a few have survived, and these are now worth quite a lot of money.) But there are many other less clear-cut examples of inaccuracies, some of which we will encounter below.

Again, some very helpful books have been written about these issues, and how the apparent difficulties presented here can be overcome, so that we can trust that our Bibles are indeed 'accurate.' If these issues are new to you, I recommend you take the time to look into them further. Very briefly stated, the solution to the first (linguistic) issue is in the work of translation, which includes the work of interpretation or hermeneutics. The solution to the second (manuscript) issue is in the work of textual criticism, which is the process of collating, comparing and evaluating manuscripts to determine the most likely original reading of each word and sentence in the Bible. These issues are important, and I will be returning to them from time to time throughout the book. But neither of them is the main focus here.

What this book is about is not first-and-foremost a human work at all, whether that's the work of a scribe, or copyist, or translator, or interpreter, or textual critic, or proofreader, or printer, or web-designer, or whatever, although most if not all of these human works are clearly vital if we are to receive an accurate Bible. Rather, above all this book is an attempt to answer the question: What is God doing in all of this? In other words, I want us to get into the 'theology' behind the history. I want to consider the works of God that ground and undergird all the human works that make up the history of the Bible and its text. Why? Because I'm convinced that will help us to trust God's 'care' of the Bible for us over the centuries. In turn, that should help us to trust God's Word, and also to trust the God who speaks to us in the Bible today. It might also help us give a reasoned account of our faith to unbelievers, in an area where it is frequently questioned.

In technical terms, then, this is a book about *the doctrine of the providential preservation of Scripture*. But don't worry—it's not a particularly technical book. The structure is quite simple. There are four chapters, and in each one, I'm going to ask (and try to answer) a question. Here are the questions:

› *Does* God preserve Scripture for us?
› *How* does God preserve Scripture for us?
› *Where* does God preserve Scripture for us?
› *Why* does God preserve Scripture for us?

In each chapter, I'm going to begin with a common 'wrong answer' to the question. I'll explain why some people give the wrong answer, and why I think it's wrong.

And then I'll try to give my own answer, drawing on teaching from the Bible and the work of scholars who have studied the Bible over the centuries. In a short conclusion at the end of the book, I'll draw the various threads of the argument together and suggest some further, practical applications of what we've learned.

So, let's begin with the most basic question of all...

1

DOES GOD PRESERVE SCRIPTURE?

'For truly, I say to you, until heaven and earth pass away, not an iota, not a dot, will pass from the Law until all is accomplished' (Matt. 5:18).

A COMMON (WRONG) ANSWER: NO.

I remember as a young Christian going along to a debate between a Christian speaker and a Muslim speaker. The debate was interesting, but after a while it became clear that the speakers were talking past one another. The Christian speaker tried to back up the things he was saying by quoting from the Bible. But the Muslim speaker responded that the text of the Bible had been corrupted, and so it was inadmissible as evidence in the discussion.

At one point, the Muslim speaker even quoted the Bible to make *his* point. He read out Jeremiah 8:8:

> How can you say, 'We are wise, and the law of the LORD is with us'? But behold, the lying pen of the scribes has made it into a lie.

He waved his finger with a triumphant flourish: 'Even the *Bible* says that the text of the Bible has been corrupted!'

I have heard this argument from Muslims many times. It is a common teaching of Islam that, while much of the Bible was indeed given as a revelation from Allah (God), the text has become corrupted over time, and additions have been made that were not original. So, the conclusion is that God has not preserved the Bible, in the way that he has preserved the Qur'ān.

There are two immediate problems with this view as commonly held by Muslims. First, in Jeremiah 8:8, the prophet is *condemning* the scribes who change the text of the Bible to suit themselves. We'll see later that there's plenty of evidence, even within the Book of Jeremiah itself, that other scribes copied and kept the true text of Scripture with painstaking care. Second, the Qur'ān itself has a complex textual history, which is not often known or acknowledged by Muslims. There's no easy comparison to be made between a supposedly pure text of the Qur'ān and a corrupt text of the Bible.[4]

Apart from the specific issues raised by Islam, others in our day deny that God has preserved the Bible. There

As Gregory R. Lanier explains, in another volume in this series, the Islamic doctrine of tahrif al-nass teaches that Jews and Christians have intentionally corrupted the text of Scripture. This idea is loosely rooted in certain verses of the Qur'an (2:75, 5:13, and 5:41). It was then more clearly developed by later writers such as al-Mahdi (744/5-785), Ibn Qutayba (828-889), and Ibn Kathir (1301-1373).

Gregory R. Lanier, *A Christian's Pocket Guide to How We Got the Bible* (Fearn: Christian Focus, 2018), 90.

are three main arguments: (1) some suggest that certain books have been 'lost'; (2) others contend that the text of the Bible has been changed deliberately, and so we can't know what it originally said: this is a bit like the Muslim argument introduced above; (3) still others argue that the original text of the Bible has simply been lost to us through the natural processes of texts decaying and disappearing, and through unintentional errors being made in copying. We'll consider these briefly here.

(1) Following the publication of Dan Brown's novel *The Da Vinci Code*⁵ many have accepted the idea—presented in the book as a sort of 'conspiracy theory'—that the Bible was changed by the Roman authorities after the Emperor Constantine made Christianity the official religion of the empire. At the very least, some suggest, certain books which might have been included in the Bible were suppressed from that time.

This story is fiction, and ought to carry a disclaimer: 'Names, characters, places, events, locales, and incidents are either the products of the author's imagination or used in a fictitious manner. Any resemblance to actual persons, living or dead, or actual events is purely coincidental.' We can be sure we have the right books in our Bibles: see Lanier's book in this series (*A Christian's Pocket Guide to How We Got the Bible*) for a persuasive presentation of the truth on this point. I'll also have a bit more to say about this question in chapter three.

(2) American New Testament scholar Bart Ehrman has pointed out that 'scribes occasionally altered the words of their sacred texts to make them more patently orthodox and to prevent their misuse by Christians who espoused aberrant views.'[6] As we'll see, Ehrman is correct on this point. There is evidence that some scribes who copied manuscripts of the Bible did make occasional changes to some of the text. But Ehrman has also asked, '[H]ow does it help us to say that the Bible is the inerrant word of God if in fact we don't have the words that God inerrantly inspired, but only the words copied by the scribes—sometimes correctly but sometimes (many times!) incorrectly?' Ehrman concludes that the Bible has *not* been preserved, so that we cannot know what was originally written (and he doesn't believe in inspiration either).

Ehrman's is not a lone voice. When I went to seminary (theological college) in Tokyo, Japan, I studied biblical Hebrew and had to write a thesis on the Old Testament. While I was doing my research, I lost count of the times that Bible commentaries, many written by professing Christians, would say something like, 'the text here is hopelessly corrupt,' or 'the original reading is lost to us.' The challenge laid down by scholars like Ehrman is important and influential (Ehrman himself in particular has written lots of popular books) and so we'll be returning to it later on.

(3) If that sounds far-removed from your experience, try opening up your Bible to 1 Samuel chapter 13. My ESV (2001 edition) reads, 'Saul was…years old when he began to reign, and he reigned for…and two years over Israel.' (Newer versions of the ESV have filled in the gaps where my Bible has […], but the problem hasn't gone away.) Why are there […] gaps in the Bible? The answer is that the Hebrew manuscripts that exist today don't have anything written here. The numbers need to be supplied, either from a translation, or from a calculation based on numbers given elsewhere. As the ESV foonote to 1 Samuel 13:1 in my Bible says, 'something may have dropped out.'

So called 'textual issues' like this can be found on almost every page of the Bible. Some can be relatively simply resolved; others (like 1 Samuel 13) are more thorny, and a good study Bible is a helpful starting-point. This is not a book about textual criticism, so I'm not going to give a long list of such issues or attempt to classify them, far less resolve them all. But suffice to say at this point that awareness of issues like these has led some to deny that God preserves Scripture for us.[7]

So, *does* God preserve Scripture for us? A good answer will take into account biblical teaching, theological reasoning (by which I mean, not going *beyond* the Bible, but thinking through—biblically—the coherence and the consequences of what the Bible says) and attention to the phenomenon of existing texts.

PRESERVATION: WHAT DOES THE BIBLE SAY?

Some evangelical biblical scholars (for example, Dan Wallace) have argued that God *does indeed* preserve the Bible, but that preservation is not a *doctrine* because the Bible doesn't teach it, and systematic theology doesn't demand it.[8] I have some sympathy with Wallace. I can't find a Bible verse that says, 'God will preserve the words of the Bible forever.' I'll admit that preservation is not as clear in the Bible as, say, inspiration. But, I think that certain verses in the Bible, taken together, amount to a strong statement about preservation. These form the foundations of the doctrine. Let's take a look at just a few of them.

> The sum of your word is truth, And every one of your righteous rules endures for ever (Ps. 119:160).

There's no word for 'endure' (or any other verb) in the Hebrew poetry here. But the Hebrew word for 'for ever' in this verse (sometimes translated 'eternally') implies endurance. The verse suggests that *all* of God's true and righteous Word is everlasting.

> The grass withers, the flower fades, but the word of our God will stand for ever (Isa. 40:8, see also 1 Pet. 1:24–25).

Here, the same Hebrew word translated 'for ever' appears. When the apostle Peter quotes this verse he uses the Greek word for 'remain' to translate the Hebrew 'stand.' The sense is the same—God's Word will not wither or fade like flowers or grass, but it will remain standing always. It is true that these Old Testament verses don't specifically mention Scripture. It is possible to argue that the references to God's 'word' here are not necessarily to his *written* Word, but refer only to his spoken promises, which will certainly be fulfilled. But in the New Testament, Jesus makes a more explicit reference to the permanence of the *written* Word of God.

'For truly, I say to you, until heaven and earth pass away, not an iota, not a dot, will pass from the Law until all is accomplished' (Matt. 5:18).

Here, in the Sermon on the Mount, Jesus is speaking about the Law of God. He is referring principally to the Books of Moses (the first five books of our Bibles) but Jews of Jesus' day could speak of the entire Old Testament as 'the Law.' What's significant for our purposes is that he speaks about 'iotas' and 'dots,' both of which were *written* phenomena.

Iota is a letter of the Greek alphabet, corresponding to *yodh*, the tenth letter of the Hebrew and Aramaic alphabets. *Yodh* is the smallest letter of the alphabet. In Jesus' day (like today) it was written like this [']. A 'dot' is literally a 'little horn' or 'hook' and refers to the tiny marks on letters of the alphabet that distinguish them from other letters.

Jesus is therefore saying that the *written* text of the Bible (at least, in this case, the Old Testament) will never 'pass away'—the same word is used in both halves of the verse, and means to 'disappear'—in this age. Later, in Matthew 24:35, he says something very similar about his own words, which at least hints that the same claim is being made for his words recorded in the New Testament. What's especially interesting is that when the originals of most of the Old Testament books were written down, the Hebrew script in use was different from that of Jesus' day and ours. In particular, we should note that in so-called 'palaeo-Hebrew' or ancient Hebrew, *yodh* [ ] wasn't an especially small letter. Jesus' rhetorical point about the Law only makes sense in a context where *yodh* is tiny, and so likely to be overlooked or counted inconsequential. That suggests that Jesus isn't so much talking about the preservation of particular shapes on the page, as about the words that the shapes (letters) represent: God's words.

It's true that Jesus isn't particularly focused on teaching us about the preservation of Scripture in the Sermon on the Mount. But it's not wrong to draw out the inferences of his teaching for our purposes: (1) until the end of this world (when heaven and earth pass away) the written Word of God will not 'pass away,' even in the slightest degree; (2) this means that, following Jesus' teaching here, the written Word of God must be in some way preserved for ever; (3) this preservation does not relate to particular letter-shapes, ink-marks, or engravings (and therefore to particular manuscripts, such as the autographs), but to the words that those shapes and marks signify.[9]

In asking what the Bible teaches about its own

The same word in modern Greek that Jesus uses for 'dot' in Matthew 5:18 means a radio or TV aerial, a tiny addition to the side of a building. I'm making a fun observation at this point, not suggesting that Jesus' words are to be understood in the light of TVs and radios.

preservation, there are other Bible passages we might consider, such as Psalm 119:89 or John 10:35. But on the basis of the evidence above we can conclude that the Bible teaches an endurance or persistence of the Word of God, and that this endurance is specifically applied by Jesus to the written Word in at least one important place in the New Testament. This teaching seems to demand some sort of preservation of Scripture.

PRESERVATION:
WHAT DOES SYSTEMATIC THEOLOGY SAY?

Talk of 'theology' makes many people—some Christians included—uncomfortable. For some, theology is by definition dry, dusty, and irrelevant. For others, theology is a move away from the Bible, into speculative ideas that dishonour God and create division in the church. Certainly, theology can be any or all of these things. But it needn't be. As is commonly observed, we all work with some kind of systematic theology—the question is: is it any good? A good systematic theology works from the biblical materials and arranges or presents them in a logical, integrated, and satisfying relationship that is faithful to the whole witness of Scripture. Prayerful and careful work of this sort, alongside other Christians, should ensure that we end up with a theology that honours God and strengthens the church.

Some doctrines are very clearly stated in Scripture. Other doctrines are formulated according to what the *Westminster Confession of Faith* (1647) calls 'good and necessary consequence' which may be deduced from Scripture.[10] As I've suggested above, the doctrine of preservation of Scripture is of the latter sort.

We might begin with one classic statement of the doctrine of preservation from the seventeenth century, which I think is a pretty good summary:

> The Old Testament in Hebrew (which was the native language of the people of God of old), and the New Testament in Greek (which, at the time of the writing of it, was most generally known to the nations), being immediately inspired by God, and, by His singular care and providence, kept pure in all ages, are therefore authentical; so as, in all controversies of religion, the Church is finally to appeal unto them. (Westminster Confession of Faith 1.8)[11]

There are three things notable about this statement for our purposes: (1) the doctrine of preservation applies to the 'authentical' Scriptures, which means those written in the original languages; (2) preservation happens by the 'providence' of God; (3) preservation is connected to inspiration. Let's unpack those ideas.

The 'Authentical' Scriptures are Preserved

The *Westminster Confession of Faith* applies preservation to the 'authentical' Scriptures. As we'll see in chapter three, it was of the utmost importance for the Reformed churches of the day to be able to define which Scriptures were 'authentical,' in response to Roman Catholic challenges. It's just as important for us today, if we confess *sola Scriptura* (Scripture alone) as our ultimate authority. Protestants defined the original-language versions of the Bible as 'authentic,' as opposed to the Latin (Vulgate) or Greek (Septuagint) translations. So, Reformed theologians and pastors commonly appealed to the 'fountains' or 'originals,' by which they meant the Old Testament in Hebrew (and Aramaic) and the New Testament in Greek.

In the seventeenth century, it was usually assumed that the autographs and the apographs (existing manuscripts) of the Bible were more or less the same. So, the authors of the *Westminster Confession of Faith* meant that both the autographs *and* the apographs were 'authentic' Scripture.[12] That doesn't mean they thought that *every* copy was *exactly* the same, and so preservation applied to every manuscript in the same way: they were aware of some variations between copies. Even so, seventeenth century Reformed Christians tended to believe that the particular manuscripts of the Bible available to them in the original languages were accurate copies of the autographs.[13] As will become clear below, it's problematic to work on the assumption that the autographs and apographs are basically identical: we have access to many more Bible manuscripts than our forebears had, and we can now see clearer than they could that the manuscripts are demonstrably rather different in places. It's therefore common in present-day evangelical doctrines of Scripture to appeal primarily to the autographs. Evangelicals typically assert that only the autographs are inspired, and so only the autographs are inerrant and authoritative.[14]

What is the relationship between the autographs and the apographs, if not one of precise identity? What exactly has been 'kept pure in all ages' by God's providence, and where can we find it? We'll consider these vital questions in detail in chapter three.

Preservation Is Providential

When we talk about 'providence' we mean, in short, *God's action in the world*.[15] One way of thinking about providence is as a kind of 'bridge' doctrine that 'links' what we say about God with what we say about God's creatures. We use the language of providence to explain how God preserves and governs the universe he has made, and how he works within that universe, in relationship with 'creaturely' causes, to bring about all his good purposes for creation, and particularly for his church. Because God himself is holy, wise and powerful, his providence exhibits these same attributes. Theologian John Webster has noted that providence is a 'ubiquitous' doctrine because it relates to everything we say about God and the world.[16] Providence begins with God in himself, in his perfect triune life as Father, Son, and Holy Spirit, because it is 'an aspect of the uncaused wonder of the overflow of God's abundant life.' God graciously gives life to creation as 'a further object of his love,' and providence 'specifies the act of creation as the beginning not simply of contingency, but also of faithful care.'[17]

When we say that God preserves Scripture *providentially*, we are saying a bit more than just *God does it*. We mean that God purposes the preservation of

Scripture for a particular reason, and in his sovereignty over all things, he works to carry out the fulfilment of his good purpose through human history. Note that we've not yet said anything about *how* God does this: that's the subject of chapter two.

Preservation Is Connected to Inspiration

In systematic theology, it is possible to demonstrate a logical connection between the doctrines of *inspiration* and *preservation*, so that one (logically) *demands* the other. Remember from the introduction to this book that 'inspiration' is the name we give to the process by which God gives all the words of the Bible to the human authors. (This is called by theologians 'plenary (=*all*) verbal (=*words*) inspiration.' *How* this happens is beyond the scope of this book.) We also need to consider the *purpose* of the Bible, in the providence of God. In other words, why has God given us the Bible in the first place? I'll have more to say about this in chapter four, but for now, consider these well-known verses from 2 Timothy:

> [T]he sacred writings [...] are able to make you wise for salvation through faith in Christ Jesus. All Scripture is breathed out by God and profitable for teaching, for reproof, for correction, and for training in righteousness, that the man of God may be competent, equipped for every good work. (2 Tim. 3:15-17)

For every one of God's people, the Bible is given for a purpose, which we might summarise as *enabling the establishment of fellowship with God.* This involves our *conversion*, as the Bible 'makes us wise for salvation through faith in Christ Jesus,' and our *growth*, as we learn from the Bible how to think and live to please God. The Bible, in other words, is *necessary* for living the Christian life.

> [Jesus] answered, 'It is written, 'Man shall not live by bread alone, but by every word that comes from the mouth of God.' (Matt. 4:4).

The necessity of the Bible's preservation may therefore be demonstrated by means of a logical syllogism, that works like this:

- God has given his people, by inspiration, all the words of the Bible. (*major premise*)
- All God's inspired words are necessary for God's people for all time. (*minor premise*)
- Therefore, God has preserved all the words of the Bible for all time. (*conclusion*)

Note that this isn't a 'proof' of the doctrine of preservation. It simply indicates that it is logically necessary, if we accept the premises. Some readers may not be familiar with the use of syllogism in articulating doctrine, but it's not unusual. For example, we might develop a support for the doctrine of biblical inerrancy syllogistically, as follows:

- God cannot err (major premise).
- The Bible is the Word of God (minor premise).
- Therefore, the Bible cannot contain error (conclusion).

Try another way of thinking about this. Imagine you're about to go on a mountaineering expedition (or, if you're like me, a gentle hillwalk). You don't know where you're going so you need a map to get you there. You've got a map (*Great!*) but half an hour into your hike, the map blows away and you're left without any guidance (*Oh no!*). You might remember bits of the map, but crucial details are missing. What use was that map in the first place? Next to none at all. The only map of any real use in such a situation is a map that stays the course with you, a map that helps you get safely to your destination without leading you astray, a map that is, in some sense 'preserved.'

The providential preservation of Scripture is the doctrine that accounts for the endurance—*for us*—of such a 'useful' and necessary book as the Bible. According to the doctrine, preservation isn't some magical quality of the written texts, like a scroll in *Harry Potter* written in indelible ink. Rather, preservation (like inspiration and illumination) is something *God does*. God, who breathed out his Word, and ensured that it was written down for us, will likewise ensure that it is preserved for us.

PRESERVATION:
WHAT DO THE EXISTING TEXTS 'SAY'?

So far, we've seen that the Bible teaches that God's written Word will endure for ever. We've also seen that, in terms of systematic theology, it is a 'good and necessary consequence' of what the Bible teaches that

God should preserve his written Word, so that we may be saved and transformed. We can conclude that God has indeed preserved Scripture for us. Because he is sovereign in all things, his preservation of Scripture is providential. But we haven't said anything yet about what that actually looks like in time and space.

Careful readers will have noticed that there are number of problems with the map analogy I used above. For one thing, it's an over-simplification. In fact, the situation is more like this (although this will strain the illustration to breaking-point): you're on a *massive* group expedition that's been going on for ages and ages. The original map is long gone, and what you've got instead is hundreds or even thousands of maps that have been copied by fellow mountaineers, most of whom are now dead. Every map is in some way a 'descendant' (copy of a copy) of the original map. Some maps are complete, others are more fragmentary. Some are older, some are newer. Some are in different languages with symbols from other countries' topographical systems. None of them match at all points. In other words, it's a bit of a muddle.

At this point, some would be tempted to go back and modify our original conclusions. Surely, given the situation 'on the ground,' we can't continue to claim that God has providentially preserved the Bible for us? Surely we must have misread the Bible, or in some way done 'bad' theology, to get us into such an apparent contradiction with what we observe 'on the ground.' Must our *inductive* reasoning (based on the phenomena we have at hand) force us to change the *deductive* reasoning (from statements or principles to logical conclusions) we have followed above?

I am convinced that we don't need to do this. Our conclusions remain sound. God *does* preserve Scripture for us, and this *is* reconcilable with the texts we have available to us. But in order to explain what is going on 'on the ground,' we need to ask another question...

2

HOW DOES GOD PRESERVE SCRIPTURE?

'Take another scroll and write on it all the former words that
were in the first scroll, which Jehoiakim the king of Judah
has burned' (Jer. 36:28).

A COMMON (WRONG) ANSWER:
BY MIRACULOUS INTERVENTION.

Christians have often claimed that God preserved
Scripture by miraculous means. Here we consider two
famous examples. The first relates particularly to the
preservation of the original-language texts of the Bible;
the second to their translation.

The Priest and the Potion

It was widely accepted by Jews in the intertestamental period (5th century BC onwards) that the autographs of the pre-exilic books of the Bible were lost. The common belief was that these had been destroyed at the time of the Babylonian exile (6th century BC). Whenever the autographs perished, we can be fairly certain that by this time they no longer existed. The 'problem' that this raised was 'solved' for both Jews and many Christians by the suggestion that God had preserved the text miraculously through Ezra the priest. (This Ezra is the same Ezra who has a book in the Bible named after him.)

The story of how this supposedly happened is found in the apocryphal (not in the Bible) book of 2 Esdras, chapter 14. In the story, God appears to Ezra in a vision, and commands him to instruct the people. Ezra is willing in principle, but he reminds God, 'The world is in darkness. Those who live in it have no light, because your Law has been burned, and so no one knows what things you have done or what works are about to come to pass' (vv. 20-21). But then Ezra comes up with an idea: 'If then I have found favour before you, send a holy spirit into me, and I will write everything that has happened

The introductions to the ESV and NIV state that they are based on the 'Masoretic Text of the Hebrew Bible found in Biblia Hebraica Stuttgartensia' (BHS). The KJV/NKJV uses the Bomberg/Ben Chayyim text, which differs from BHS in fewer than a dozen places. Likewise, the modern Greek Orthodox translations of the OT are based directly on 4th–5th century Greek codices, not on intermediate translations.

in the world from the beginning, the things that were written in your Law, so that human beings can find the path, and those who want to live in the last days may live' (v. 22). God agrees to Ezra's plan, and he gives Ezra a miraculous cup to drink, 'full of something like water, but its colour was like fire.' For the next forty days, fired up by his spiritual energy drink, Ezra dictates day and night the words that God gives him to five specially-selected men, who write down everything Ezra dictates to them, 'in characters that they didn't know.' In other words, according to this story, it doesn't matter that we don't have the original autograph of the book of Genesis. Thanks to Ezra and his fiery potion (and of course a divine miracle) we have an exact replica of it (and the rest of the Old Testament too).

To our minds, the word 'apocryphal' (in the modern sense, meaning 'of doubtful authenticity') is a perfect description for stories like this one. But many Christians have believed this story, or some version of it at least.[18] The story had powerful explanatory force. It was used to reassure the doubters and confound the critics. It helped Christians to understand how the autographs of the Bible could be lost, and yet God could still have preserved his Word, by means of a great miracle.

The Legend of the Seventy

Another widely-accepted tale of miraculous preservation of the Bible specifically concerns its translation. The so-called 'Legend of the Seventy' is an account (well-known in the early church) of how the Hebrew Old Testament was translated into Greek in the third century BC. This legend was based on a Jewish story about the so-called *Septuagint* (Greek for 'seventy') translation of the Old Testament. The story is of dubious origin, and it went through various versions and embellishments as it was transmitted. But in the early church, nobody seems to have known it was a legend. Irenaeus, who lived in the second century AD, records his version of the story in *Against Heresies*. Following the story as he had learned it, Irenaeus says that the Egyptian king Ptolemy (285–247 BC) commissioned the translation of the Bible for his library in Alexandria. He tells how the Jews sent seventy elders 'thoroughly skilled in the Scriptures and in both the languages' (Hebrew and Greek) to Alexandria from Jerusalem. Irenaeus records what Ptolemy did next:

> [W]ishing to test them individually, and fearing lest they might perchance, by taking counsel together, conceal the truth in the Scriptures, by their interpretation, [the king] separated them from each other, and commanded them all to write the same translation. He did this with respect to all the books. But when they came together in the same place before Ptolemy, and each of them compared his own inter- pretation with that of every other, God was indeed glorified, and the Scriptures were acknowledged as truly divine. For all of them read out the common translation [which they had prepared] in the very same words and the very same names, from beginning to end, so that even the Gentiles present perceived that the Scriptures had been interpreted by the inspiration of God. (*Against Heresies*, III. 21.2)

From a story like this, we can see that Christians like Irenaeus believed the Greek *Septuagint* to have been 'inspired' by God, like the Hebrew and Aramaic originals of the Old Testament. What is remarkable about the 'Legend of the Seventy' is that some Christians—in the West as well as in the East—accepted a version of it as a basically true account, right through the Reformation period and well into the seventeenth century.[19] Why was this legend, with its appeal to a divine miracle, so popular? The answer is probably that it gave Christians confidence that God had not left the transmission and translation of the Bible text to chance. Rather, he had worked in miraculous ways to preserve the text, so that they could be sure that nothing had been 'lost in translation.'

The question remains: *How* does God preserve Scripture for us? In this chapter, I'm going to argue that God does this—for the most part—through his 'ordinary providence.' It's not (usually) 'miraculous,' but if we understand it, it's every bit as sure and as awe-inspiring.

> How great are your works, O LORD!
> Your thoughts are very deep! (Ps. 92:5)

Even if we classify stories like these as mere 'legends,' is there really no place for the miraculous in the preservation of Scripture? And if we lose the element of miracle, what account can we give in its place?

WHAT IS A MIRACLE, ANYWAY?

I live near to the Scottish National Gallery of Modern Art in Edinburgh. In the grounds of the gallery, there's a striking sculpture made of scaffolding and electric lights by the artist Nathan Coley. The lights spell out in large letters the slogan 'THERE WILL BE NO MIRACLES HERE.' Whatever Coley's intentions, his sculpture expresses well the secular assumptions of Enlightenment thought. Another son of Edinburgh, the empiricist philosopher David Hume (1711-1776), defined a miracle as a violation of the natural law by the will of God, and then famously proceeded to argue that miracles do not—and cannot—happen.

As a Christian, I believe in miracles, both as theoretical possibility and as historical fact. But what exactly do I believe in? And what do I mean when I say that the preservation of Scripture is not miraculous? We need a definition of 'miracle.' 'Miracle' is not a Bible word, as such. The word that sometimes gets translated 'miracle' in the Old Testament (*môphēt*) means a 'wonder.' In the New Testament it's a word that literally means 'powerful deed' (*dynamis*). *All* God's deeds are powerful and wonderful. But I still think there's a helpful, specific use for the term 'miracle.'

David Hume may have come to the wrong conclusion (his worldview precluded the possibility of miracles before he had begun) but his definition is actually pretty good.[20] The most useful definitions of 'miracles' draw a distinction between two different ways that God works 'providentially.' Remember from chapter one that 'providence' means *God's action in the world*. All of providence is God's work. And everything that happens in the world happens within the sovereignty of God, which means that everything falls under God's powerful, holy and wise providence.

But as we read the Bible we start to see that God works providentially in two different ways. Sometimes, he works through what theologians call 'ordinary' providence. (In English today, 'ordinary' means something like 'normal,' or 'usual,' but the Latin word *ordinarius* that's behind the theological term means 'rule.' God's 'ordinary' providence is his providence according to the rules or laws he has established.) In the work of 'ordinary' providence, there's no suspending or altering natural laws. God works through 'ordinary' means. The storm that brought Paul's ship to the island of Malta (Acts 27) is a good example of God's ordinary providence in action. God, as sovereign over the wind and the waves (and everything else) sent the storm that wrecked the ship, but he didn't need to break any natural laws to do so. So much for 'ordinary' providence: 'THERE WILL BE NO MIRACLES HERE'—but not because God is not active or involved. He *is*, but his involvement is according to (his own) rules.

In contrast, God's 'extraordinary' providence (literally, his 'outside-the-rules' providence) is, by definition, a suspension or alteration of natural laws in particular circumstances. When Paul came ashore on Malta, and in the very next chapter was bitten by a poisonous snake (Acts 28), the islanders expected him to die. When he didn't, they attributed this to a miracle, and I think Luke (the writer of *Acts*) wants us to see Paul's deliverance as miraculous too. The pagans on the island thought Paul must be a god (Luke gives us a laugh at their expense): *we* know that the one, true God was at work to protect his apostle. When he works by means of such 'extraordinary' providence, God 'breaks the rules.' Events that happen according to 'extraordinary' providence are rightly called 'miracles.'

God is constantly at work in our world. But his mode of operating is different, depending on the particular situation. Sometimes he acts directly and miraculously, by extraordinary providence. At all other times, he acts indirectly, through the rules that he has established, by ordinary providence.

Armed with our definition, we can now attempt to account for the different things God does. For example, by the definition put forward in this chapter, *your* birth was not a miracle (though it was still a wonderful and powerful work of God). But *Jesus'* birth *was* a miracle: he was born of a virgin.

What about the preservation of Scripture? We must admit that God *could have* done this miraculously, by means of extraordinary providence. On Christian faith principles, either of the 'legends' with which this

The question in distinguishing ordinary and extraordinary providence is not: Is God at work? Fundamental to the biblical worldview is that God is always at work (John 5:17, Psalm 121:4). We should recognise his hand in everything that happens, even if we sometimes cannot understand why particular things happen.

chapter began *could have happened*. Much stranger things happened *in* and *according to* Scripture, and we believe them for sure. As we've seen, many (perhaps most) Christians *did* believe these legends, for hundreds of years. I think they were wrong, but their position has this going for it: it's better than David Hume's. God is all-powerful, and can do as he pleases. He could have preserved Scripture miraculously. The question is, *did he?* As in the previous chapter, we'll begin our investigation in the Bible itself.

BIBLE MANUSCRIPTS GET DESTROYED: GOD IS SOVEREIGN

Jeremiah chapter 36 contains one of the most dramatic scenes in the Old Testament. The story is fast-paced and full of tension. The chapter begins as the LORD speaks words to Jeremiah the prophet and tells him to write them down. Jeremiah dictates the LORD's words to his secretary, Baruch, who writes them down on a scroll.

Jeremiah then tells Baruch to go and read the scroll to the people in the Temple in Jerusalem, because he himself is 'banned from going to the house of the LORD' (v.5). Baruch obeys, and he reads the scroll aloud on the day of a great fast when all the people are gathered in the Temple. So far, so good.

The problems begin when King Jehoiakim of Judah (a bad king, according to his write-up in *Kings* and *Chronicles*) hears about this. Jehoiakim isn't there at the Temple when Baruch is reading the scroll, but his

Jeremiah 36 is a great example of one way in which God inspires Scripture, and how it actually comes to be written down. It is only one example, though: not all Scripture was inspired in the same way.

henchmen/officials are, and they hear the message. It's a message of judgment and coming 'disaster' (v. 3). The officials summon Baruch and confirm that the message is indeed from Jeremiah the prophet. Jeremiah is already *persona non grata* in the eyes of the king, and this new message is not calculated to improve royal-prophetic relations. A storm is brewing! So the officials suggest to Baruch that he make himself scarce: 'Go and hide, you and Jeremiah, and let no one know where you are.' (v. 19)

No doubt taking a deep breath, the officials make their report to the king, but perhaps even they don't expect a reaction quite like the one they see:

> Then the king sent Jehudi [one of his officials] to get the scroll, and he took it from the chamber of Elishama the secretary. And Jehudi read it to the king and all the officials who stood beside the king. It was the ninth month, and the king was sitting in the winter house, and there was a fire burning in the fire pot before him. As Jehudi read three or four columns, the king would cut them off with a knife and throw them into the fire in the fire pot, until the entire scroll was consumed in the fire that was in the fire pot. Yet neither the king nor any of his servants who heard all these words was afraid, nor did they tear their garments. (Jer. 36:21-24)

The Hebrew of Jeremiah 36 is emphatic—it was the king *himself* who did all the cutting and burning. Evil

Jehoiakim cared nothing for the Word of the LORD or for the LORD's prophet. (Jehoiakim got his comeuppance later on as he died an ignominious death in exile in Babylon.) He held the written Word in such contempt that he burned it to keep himself warm, and he would have seized Jeremiah if he could, but for the LORD preserving the prophet's life (v. 26). God preserved his prophet. But what about his written Word? Well, God told Jeremiah to start again:

> Now after the king had burned the scroll with the words that Baruch wrote at Jeremiah's dictation, the word of the LORD came to Jeremiah: 'Take another scroll and write on it all the former words that were in the first scroll, which Jehoiakim the king of Judah has burned. [...] Then Jeremiah took another scroll and gave it to Baruch the scribe, the son of Neriah, who wrote on it at the dictation of Jeremiah all the words of the scroll that Jehoiakim king of Judah had burned in the fire. And many similar words were added to them. (Jer. 36:27–28, 32)

One thing this story makes clear is that it's quite possible for written texts—even Scripture texts—that contain words from God to be destroyed. That doesn't surprise God, or put him on the back foot. He is sovereign, and he has a plan to preserve his Word. In Jeremiah's case, God's plan is simple: he tells Jeremiah to write it out again, and Jeremiah dictates another scroll to Baruch. Was this a miracle? The text of Jeremiah 36 doesn't seem to suggest so. The new scroll did contain 'all the words' that were in the first scroll, but it wouldn't be surprising if Jeremiah (and Baruch) had remembered them. When we're told that 'many similar words were added' that doesn't mean that Jeremiah and Baruch came up with a new and improved version of the oracle that Jehoiakim had burned. It simply means that other, separate, oracles from God were included. Many years later, at the end of a long and complicated historical process, they would form part of the book we know as the Book of Jeremiah.

The inspiration of Scripture is often miraculous and mysterious. How did Jeremiah *get* 'words from the LORD'? We don't know. The preservation of Scripture, on the other hand, is mostly meticulous and mundane. It involves the exercise of human faculties such as memory and transcription, and such faculties are certainly fallible. For the most part God's preservation of Scripture proceeds without his miraculous intervention. The processes are not mysterious. But that does not mean that God is not at work. I am certainly not suggesting that God inspires the Bible and then somehow 'hands over' the text to natural processes with which he is not concerned, rather like the God of Deism.[21] Rather, in his ordinary providence, God is sovereign over all things, and he acts in and through natural, creaturely causes, to ensure that his Word is preserved for all time.

What this story helps us to see is that God's preservation of Scripture is not tied to particular texts or scrolls. We've already seen in chapter one that it's not tied to particular shapes of letters on a page either. It is tied to divinely-given words—words God has ordained for writing down and preservation for the benefit of his people and as a testimony to the world, forever.

THE WORD OF GOD IS PRESERVED:
GOD IS SOVEREIGN

The Bible itself assumes that the Bible will be copied. For example, the kings of Israel were commanded to make their own, personal copy of God's law (Deut. 17:18-20). The priests were to be on hand while the copy was made (v.18), presumably to check that it was copied correctly. But there's no hint of the miraculous in this process.

Even if we don't call the preservation of the Bible a 'miracle,' we should still recognise that it is a wonderful work of God. There's something amazing about the preservation of Scripture—something that should cause us to sit up and take notice. After all, King Jehoiakim wasn't the only historical leader who has tried to destroy the Bible. Furthermore, the destruction of texts of Scripture hasn't always been intentional or malicious. Simon Keynes relates the story of the 'Cotton Genesis,' which was once one of the most beautiful illuminated (illustrated) Greek manuscripts of the first book of the Bible. In 1731, this biblical manuscript was almost totally destroyed in a fire, which nearly claimed even more valuable treasures. As Keynes tells the story, citing contemporary accounts, the renowned classical scholar Richard Bentley visited London on business, and

> naturally enough, he came with his wife to stay at their son's suitably commodious apartments in Ashburnham House. A 'goode fire' had been made for Dr Bentley's comfort 'in a Stove chimney under the Library'; and [...] Bentley himself

had been unsure 'whether he did not leave the Blower on the Stove when he went to Bed'. Whatever the case, it seems that a wooden jamb in the chimney ignited, transmitting the fire to the library on the floor above. The great scholar was woken from his slumbers 'by his Ladys Coughing', and 'perceiv'd a Smell of wood smoke'; whereupon he appears to have grabbed the fifth-century Codex Alexandrinus [a very important, early NT manuscript] from the shelves of the Royal Library, and made good his escape in nightgown and wig, with the manuscript under his arms.[22]

This story vividly illustrates both the potential perils facing fragile texts, as well as the 'ordinary providence' that is represented by Mrs Bentley's cough. (One wonders what she said to her husband afterwards: on the face of it, he seems to have been more concerned to save the manuscript from the flames than his wife.)

John Calvin argued that the providential preservation of the books of the Bible throughout the ups-and-downs of Israelite history was a testimony to their divine origin.[23] That sounds about right. The Israelites went through an exodus, a conquest, civil wars, rebellions, sieges and an exile, and yet God preserved the books of the Old Testament. Calvin's comment suggests a helpful parallel: the preservation of Scripture through Israel's history is similar in many ways to the preservation of David's royal dynasty through Israel's history. Both were necessary for the salvation of God's people, for Jesus the Messiah was to be born of David's line.

There were times when the survival of David's dynasty

hung on a knife-edge. Think of little Joash (a.k.a. Jehoash), hidden away in the Temple for six years while wicked Queen Athaliah 'arose and destroyed all the royal family' (2 Kings 11:1). Joash was the only one left of David's royal line, but his life was preserved, and he went on to be both king of Israel and ancestor of Jesus. It wasn't exactly a 'miracle'—no natural laws were broken. Joash wasn't fed by ravens like Elijah; he was looked after by his nurse. The Bible doesn't specifically say that 'God did it.' But that's the only conclusion left to the reader.

Surely there were times also when the survival of Scripture hung on a knife-edge. What if, for example, Tychicus, who probably delivered Paul's letter to the Colossians (2:7-8), had never made it to his destination? Or what if the early Christians had decided not to include some of the books that were meant to be in the Bible, and they had fallen out of the canon, and out of use? We could come up with a whole list of *what ifs*. But through all of these, history and faith teach us that God preserved Scripture for us. He is sovereign in all things. And that should give us confidence that he has fulfilled his purpose.

We've seen in this chapter that God preserved the

Joash is one of four kings of Judah who don't appear in Matthew's genealogy of Jesus, in Matthew 1:2-17. Even so, there's no disputing that he was a direct ancestor of Jesus. Matthew has 'telescoped' his genealogy, missing out certain individuals for his own purposes. (This was common practice in ancient genealogical reckoning.) Interestingly, one of the other kings left out by Matthew is Jehoiakim, whom we've already encountered in Jeremiah 36.

Bible for us by means of his ordinary providence, and that should give us cause to wonder and be thankful. But lots of questions remain. Particularly, once we accept that God has preserved the Bible, and that he has done this by his ordinary providence, we might ask: *where exactly is that Bible that God has preserved, and how do we access it?* These questions are the subject of the next chapter.

3

WHERE DOES GOD PRESERVE SCRIPTURE?

I warn everyone who hears the words of the prophecy of
this book: if anyone adds to them, God will add to him the
plagues described in this book, and if anyone takes away
from the words of the book of this prophecy, God will take
away his share in the tree of life and in the holy city, which
are described in this book. (Rev. 22:18-19)

A COMMON (WRONG) ANSWER:
IN SOME PARTICULAR MANUSCRIPTS.

Let's sum up where we've got to so far. God preserves
Scripture for us, by his ordinary providence. A miracle
would be so much 'neater,' but what we actually find
looks more like a muddle than a miracle. Faced with this
apparent muddle, some Christians have tried to tie up
the loose ends, and concluded that God has preserved
his Word in one or more particular manuscripts or

translations. There are various versions of this idea, which we'll consider briefly here.

Eastern Orthodoxy

The churches of the East use the (Greek) Septuagint translation of the Old Testament in their liturgy. According to Eastern Orthodoxy, the Septuagint is a divinely-inspired translation, and this is the text that has been preserved by the church, according to God's providence. As we've seen, a similar view was not uncommon in the early church and even among some western Christians in later times as well.

Roman Catholicism

At the time of the Reformation, the church of Rome adopted the Latin Vulgate translation of the Bible (which was first made in the late 4th century) as its authoritative version of Scripture.[24] In debates with Protestants,

The Bible does not teach that the church is given authority to select a particular text and declare that text of Scripture to be 'official' or 'authoritative.' In this respect, Roman Catholics would disagree. Their position is precisely that the church does have such authority. Among other Bible passages, Rome commonly appeals to 1 Timothy 3:15 to support its position. In that verse, Paul refers to the 'church of the living God' as 'a pillar and buttress of the truth.' For Roman Catholics, the church comes before Scripture and therefore in a sense the church 'gives birth' to the Bible—as 'pillar and buttress of the truth,' the church has the right to declare which text of Scripture is authoritative.

Catholic apologists argued that the Protestant appeal to *sola Scriptura* (=Scripture alone) was meaningless because the Protestants could not specify *which* Scripture text they were talking about.

In response, the Protestant Reformers argued that Rome had misunderstood Paul's meaning. They said that although the church pre-existed the writing down of (most of) the Bible, nevertheless the church is still the creation of the Word of God, which was later written down. As 'pillar and buttress of the truth,' the church has, under God, the important role of preserving Scripture: defending, protecting, and living in obedience to the Word of God. But the church is always the servant of the Word, whether that Word is written or spoken.

King James Only-ism

Some fundamentalist Protestant Christians (particularly in the USA) believe that the King James Version (or KJV [1611], sometimes called the 'Authorised Version') is the version of the Bible that God has specially preserved. There are varieties of this position, as some argue that it is only the Hebrew and Greek text *behind* the KJV (for the NT, the so called *textus receptus*, or received text) that has been preserved, while others take the view that the English words of the KJV themselves are divinely-inspired. A particularly radical type of KJV Only-ism asserts that the KJV in English is God's final revelation, which supersedes, and may even be used to correct, existing Hebrew or Greek texts.

The Majority Text View

In recent years, a small but significant number of Bible scholars have supported the view that the text of the New Testament which God has preserved is the so-called 'majority text.' Basically this is the type (or 'family') of text that is found in the highest number of existing manuscripts of the New Testament. This is not the place to discuss text-types and other technical issues of textual criticism. But the key belief for proponents of this view is that God has made it clear to us which text is the 'right' one by ensuring the numerical supremacy of that particular type of text.

The Hebrew Vowel-Points Controversy

In the seventeenth century, a controversy over exactly *where* God had preserved his Word led to some well-known Reformed scholars and pastors taking a position that subsequent scholarship has clearly demonstrated to have been a mistake. They argued that the preservation (and inspiration) of the Old Testament extended even to the 'vowel-points' of the Hebrew text. The history of this controversy is not well known today, but I want to introduce it here because it illustrates some of the points I'm making about what providential preservation necessarily entails, and what it does *not* entail.

A little background explanation is required. The Hebrew text of the Old Testament was originally consonantal only: the vowels needed to be 'supplied' by the reader. Many centuries later, the vowels were added to the text by the Masoretes, by means of a system of dots and dashes that symbolised the intended vowel sounds. These sounds were, of course, crucial to establishing the intended reading, and meaning, of the text.

By way of illustration, here's the first verse of Genesis 1 in the consonantal text. You read it from right to left:[25]

בראשית ברא אלהים את השמים ואת הארץ:

And here's what it looks like with the vowels:

בְּרֵאשִׁית בָּרָא אֱלֹהִים אֵת הַשָּׁמַיִם וְאֵת הָאָרֶץ:

How could such tiny marks have provoked a great controversy? How could any Christians believe that the salvation of souls might depend on minute textual details like these?

The sixteenth-century Reformers (such as Luther and Calvin) had been content to affirm that God had inspired and then providentially preserved the Bible, without specifying in detail what this had involved. But later Protestants had to respond carefully to Roman Catholic claims that their doctrine of the sufficiency and authority of Scripture was incoherent, given that in the Protestant understanding there was no single authoritative text or translation. In essence the Roman Catholic challenge to

The Masoretes were a group of Jewish scribes who worked to preserve the text of the Old Testament between the 6th and the 10th centuries AD.

the Protestants was: *Show us your authoritative text!* (As we've seen, the Roman church had decided on the Latin Vulgate as its 'authentical' text of Scripture.)

When some Protestant scholars began to suggest that the Hebrew vowel-points were not original (as had been generally presumed) but were in fact the creation of the Masoretes centuries after Christ,[26] this provoked not a little embarrassment. A doctrine of *sola Scriptura* that in practice appeared to depend on precisely the 'tradition' of the Masoretes (unbelieving Jews!) did not on the surface sound very convincing in debates with Rome. This also provoked a conservative reaction. Reformed leaders like John Owen argued that God must have both inspired the vowel-points, *and* preserved them from the time of writing the autographs to the present day. Otherwise, in Owen's view, Scripture could no longer be 'sufficient'— the church would depend in some sense on human traditions in order to ascertain the Bible's meaning, and therefore Scripture's authority would be compromised.

Owen's two-fold mistake—apart from the historical inaccuracy concerning the origin of the vowel-points— was to assume that (1) preservation (and inspiration) related to the physical and orthographical phenomena of a written text, and (2) only the true people of God could preserve the written Word of God.

In respect of (1) both the doctrine of preservation and that of inspiration refer to *words*. Inspiration is *verbal*, and it is the *words* of Scripture that God has preserved. The original Hebrew text of Genesis may not have had vowel-points, but the words it was made up of certainly had vowels, or they wouldn't have made any sense. These sounds have been preserved, or are able to be reconstructed so that we can ascertain the intended meaning, by means of various traditions (including the tradition of the Masoretes) and translations, and so we have very good reason to believe that we can access the original author's intended words. A doctrine of providential preservation demands that the words of Scripture must have been preserved, but it doesn't tell us by whom (on the human level), nor does it confine us to a particular manuscript or text-type.

In respect of (2) there is no reason to assume that God cannot use unbelievers, such as the Masoretes, to preserve his written Word. Indeed, one of the editors of the latest critical edition of the Old Testament (*Biblia Hebraica Quinta*) is a Mormon professor from Brigham Young University.[27] Can God use a (non-Trinitarian) Mormon to work on the textual criticism of a Hebrew text that will likely form the basis of future Bible translations across the world? History suggests that he can.

There is something attractive about the various propositions outlined above. They each, in their own way, attempt to remove some of the uncertainty we might feel about where to find the divinely-preserved text of Scripture. I'm not going to engage further with any of these views directly. Rather, I'm going to present what I think is the correct position positively, and try to demonstrate its superiority to alternative views.

TOWARDS A SOLUTION

Here's a brief summary of my position: *God has preserved his words by the existing 'manuscript tradition' of the canonical Old and New Testaments, and he guides his church so that she can always hear the divine words she needs, and can grow in confidence in those words as the Spirit leads her.*

To unpack and defend this position, I'm going to argue in this chapter that God, in his sovereignty, leads people (not always 'his' people!) to make and keep copies of (i) the 'canon' of Scripture, (ii) the Old Testament in its original languages, (iii) the New Testament in its original language, and (iv) Bible translations. Discovering the *location* of God's preservation of Scripture for us involves all four of these elements.[28]

1. The Canon

How do we know which books should be in the Bible? Who decides? How do we know we've got the correct ones? This brings us to the question of the 'canon' of Scripture. The issues involved go beyond the scope of this book, and if this is a topic you'd like to follow up, the 'suggestions for further reading' section at the back offers further reading suggestions.

'Canon,' by the way, means 'measuring rod' or 'rule.' It's a standard by which we determine what is 'in' and what is 'out.' The canon of Scripture, for Christians everywhere, is the 66 books that make up our Bibles. Some churches, like the Roman Catholic church, have a *deutero*-canon, or 'second' canon. This consists of the books that Protestants typically refer to as the 'apocrypha.' But Roman Catholics and Protestants alike agree on the basic canon of Scripture. That fact is in itself quite remarkable.

The historical process by which the canon of Scripture came to be has been well documented elsewhere, so I won't repeat that here.[29] Instead, with our focus on *God's* purposes and *God's* work I'm going to draw briefly on the excellent work of biblical scholar Meredith Kline (d. 2007) who has demonstrated that the Bible itself teaches the *necessity* of a canon for the church.[30] Kline argues persuasively that, because God's relationship with his people is 'covenantal' in nature (*i.e.* God makes covenants with us), such a relationship *by definition* demands a written covenant deed or treaty. The treaty specifies the parties to the covenant, maps out its history, and lays out the stipulations according to which the covenant will be enforced and lived out. It's this covenant treaty that we call the 'canon' of Scripture. The shape of the relationship demands a canon. Kline shows how the Old Testament contains exactly the same elements as ancient Near Eastern suzerain-vassal treaties, and how the Old Testament then 'tees up' the expectation of a New Testament to complete and fulfil itself.

In short, the church without the Bible is an impossibility. If we accept Kline's argument, we are committed to the view that God himself *must* lead and guide the church into acknowledging and preserving the canon of Scripture, correctly. Following the argument made so far in this book, I want to argue that the 'selection' of the books of the biblical canon was not *just* a human work (although it was certainly a human work, if a largely passive work of *acceptance, assent,* and *recognition*). It was also God's work. In fact, it was part of his work of preserving Scripture, by his ordinary providence. So, we can have confidence that we have the 'correct' books in our Bibles. None are missing. None are 'interlopers' that need to be weeded out. Each one has its place in the complete, written Word of God. Once again, the fact that the church did, historically, select the books that are in the canon (rejecting others in the process) doesn't mean that the church is 'above' Scripture. In the human act of determining the canon, the church, led by the Holy Spirit, acknowledges, accepts and submits.

God has preserved Scripture for us in the canon. This fact itself has encouraged the church to copy and pass on Scripture with sufficient accuracy. The solemn warning at the end of the Bible not to add to or take away from

When we talk about a work being both divine and human at the same time, we're using the language of what philosophers call 'double agency.' How that works will have to be the subject of another book! But note that it's not a 'zero-sum game,' so that a particular work is thought of as, say, 80% divine and 20% human. A biblical view of divine and human agency (action) understands these as compatible and operating at different 'levels' without contradicting one another. Rather, human agency is genuine, meaningful, and morally-accountable, precisely because the work of God is its ground. The preservation of Scripture is a great example of this: it is both God's work and a human work, and there is no conflict or competition between these two agencies.

the words of the book does not apply only to the Book of Revelation in which it is found, but indirectly to the whole Bible. Because of the canon, the church knows which books are to be kept, and has laboured to preserve them under God's direction.

2. The Old Testament

The earliest printed text of the Old Testament in Hebrew and Aramaic was produced in Soncino, Italy, in A.D. 1488. That means that, for nearly three thousand years, the Old Testament was preserved and transmitted by *hand* copying alone. As we've noted, human scribes being *human* scribes (with no miracles equivalent to inspiration) means that mistakes and variations have inevitably crept into the manuscripts. There were probably multiple different versions and 'families' of text-types in the Old Testament period itself.

But evangelical Old Testament text expert Ellis Brotzman explains how, by A.D. 135 at the latest, the Jews had settled on a 'single and authoritative text type.'[31] This text type is broadly in agreement with what later came to be called the 'Masoretic' text. If you read from a modern English translation of the Old Testament (such as the ESV, NIV etc.) it is based on the Masoretic text.

Scribal errors and other variations in the Masoretic text are far fewer than we might expect from a text tradition of such antiquity. This is mainly because the Jewish scribes who copied the text were committed to transmitting it as accurately as humanly possible. They took such painstaking care because they had a very high view of the written Word of God. One piece of evidence for this is found in my printed Hebrew Old Testament (which is based on a manuscript of the Masoretic text known as the Leningrad Codex) at the end of the book of Deuteronomy. The Masoretes have recorded there some 'statistics' about the text. We're told that the sum total of verses in the Torah (the first five books of the Old Testament) is 5,845. This is made up of 167 paragraphs, 79,856 words, and 400,945 letters. It was common practice for completed copies to be subjected to a stringent process of checking and letter-counting. Manuscripts that failed the test—by even a single letter—were supposedly destroyed.

Until the mid-twentieth century, it was hard to be sure how well the Masoretic text really had been preserved. That's because the oldest manuscript copies of the Old Testament available dated from the 10th and 11th centuries A.D., thousands of years after some books of the Old Testament were first written.

But, in 1947, a spectacular discovery was made: the so-called 'Dead Sea Scrolls.' Among the many documents found in caves in the Judean desert, all dating from c.250 B.C–c.65 A.D., were more than 225 biblical manuscripts. The great majority of these scrolls *support* the Masoretic text of the Old Testament. They demonstrate the amazing precision with which, in the providence of God, the Masoretic text was copied for a thousand years.

Even so, if we were to argue that God has preserved the Old Testament *perfectly* in the Masoretic text, we would end up making the same mistake with which this chapter begins—limiting preservation to *one* particular text-type. The Masoretic text *is* remarkably well-preserved, but almost all evangelical scholars believe that it can be corrected in places. Broadly speaking, there are three main types of corrections.

- First, there is 'revocalisation.' As we've seen, the Old Testament was originally written in consonants only. The vowels were added into the text later on. 'Revocalisation' is when different vowels are attached to the consonantal text, giving a different meaning. For example, if we only had the English consonants 'HVN', we might not know whether the author intended 'heaven' or 'haven' or even 'Havana'. In my ESV, there are two examples of revocalisation in Psalm 109, verses 17 and 18.

- Second, corrections to the Masoretic text might be made according to the 'ancient versions' or translations of the Old Testament. Sometimes these translations reflect a likely ancient original reading that was lost in most or all of the surviving Hebrew texts. Ancient versions include the Septuagint (Greek), the Syriac and the Vulgate (Latin). ESV has an example of this kind of correction in Psalm 97:11. In the footnote, 'Jerome' refers to the Latin translation, because Jerome was the translator.

- Third, sometimes, corrections are made according to the Dead Sea Scrolls. Isaiah 21:8 in the ESV is an example.

Again, as this isn't a book about textual criticism, I'm not going to go into details about these verses and the issues involved. I'd just like you to notice that the Hebrew Masoretic text *can* be amended, but not randomly or arbitrarily so. In each case, scholars use the texts that have been handed down to try to render most accurately the original reading. We should therefore see God's providential preservation of the Old Testament as including *all* of the textual evidence available to us. This sum total of textual evidence is called the 'manuscript tradition.' God has determined what is needed for his people to have a sufficient (if not perfect) access to his Word, and has ensured that it has been handed down to us.

'Tradition' literally means something that has been 'handed down.' The manuscript 'tradition' consists of all the texts of the Bible that we have received from previous generations. New manuscripts (especially of the New Testament) continue to be discovered.

3. The New Testament

There are over 5,000 preserved copies of portions of the New Testament in Greek, its original language. There are many more early manuscripts in translation. Unlike the Old Testament, there is exactly the kind of muddle we might expect from 1,400 years of hand-copying of manuscripts, by all kinds of people, often during times when the church faced 'many dangers, toils and snares.'[32] There are, thankfully, some great exceptions, but the New Testament wasn't always copied with the care and precision we might have wished for. Some classically awful examples have survived. My favourite is from a manuscript of the four Gospels, known as Codex 109, which you can go and see in the British Museum. It must have been copied from a text that had Luke's genealogy of Jesus (Luke 3:12-38) in two columns. The not-too-clever scribe, instead of reading *down* each column, copied *across* from one column to the other. The result makes everyone the son of the wrong father. Worse, the last person in the list is not God, but someone called Phares, who becomes the father of the entire human race. God is listed as the son of Aram.[33]

Not all the variants in New Testament manuscripts come from mistakes. Some scribes felt free to 'harmonise' texts, so that, for example, Matthew, Mark and Luke were made to say exactly the same thing. (Given the typical scribe's familiarity with the Bible, such harmonisations may even have been *un*intentional. If you've ever tried to memorise Bible verses you'll know how the particular version you've remembered can stick in your mind, and that's not a bad thing.) Others seem to have amended texts for doctrinal reasons, although we can't always be sure why, and it's hard to prove in particular cases. We already noted this point about scribal changes in chapter one as an objection made by critical scholar Bart Ehrman, who rejects both the inspiration and providential preservation of the Bible. Ehrman thinks this means that we can't access the original wording.

But it's important to understand that it's usually possible to tell whether a manuscript is generally reliable or not. No-one is likely to consider Codex 109 a useful witness to what Luke originally wrote in his genealogy of Jesus. If one manuscript makes Matthew, Mark and Luke say the same thing, when most manuscripts have them saying different things, it's pretty likely that the 'harmonised' version is secondary.

So, textual criticism of the New Testament certainly isn't simple, but it's also by no means a shot in the dark. Not only is it possible to make general judgments about the quality and reliability of New Testament manuscripts, textual critics are able to work out with extremely high levels of certainty what the New Testament originally said at the level of individual chapters, verses and words. Text critic Peter Gurry has recently suggested that a 'reasonable estimate' for the number of textual variants in the Greek New Testament is about 500,000.[34] Half a million variants? The number sounds large. But Gurry's reading of the data leads him to conclude that 'the number reflects the frequency with which scribes copied more than their infidelity in doing so.'[35] We need not be worried about this large number of variants. The verses of the NT where there is real uncertainty about what was originally written are comparatively few. Dan Wallace puts the number of variants that are both 'meaningful' and 'viable' at less than 1% of the total.[36] We know exactly where these 'uncertain' places are, and not one of them affects the status of a major doctrine. It's not as though half our manuscripts say 'Jesus *is* Lord' and the other half say 'Jesus *isn't* Lord.' Even where there's a complex textual issue, the general sense of the verse in question is in most cases the same.

I must admit that there are some difficult, unresolved questions about certain verses in the New Testament, like the end of Mark's Gospel, or the story of the woman caught in adultery (John 7:53-8:11). These verses are often printed in a different font in modern Bible translations, or included in brackets, because it's doubtful whether they were part of the original book. It's hard to give a definitive answer to these questions now, but that doesn't mean that further scholarship or manuscript discoveries won't reveal an answer to us in the future.

Evangelical scholars do disagree on whether God has preserved the words of Scripture *in* the existing manuscript tradition (so that the original wording has always been preserved in at least one manuscript), or God has preserved his words *by* the existing manuscript tradition (so that in certain, rare, cases the original reading *may* have dropped out of the tradition, but it may be restored by considering all the evidence in existing manuscripts). Such restoration is called 'conjectural emendation.' This is a complicated debate, but on balance I tend to agree with the latter position, which is a common approach in the textual criticism of other ancient texts. However, it is also true that there are *far* more existing manuscripts of the New Testament than of any comparable work of ancient literature, and many of them are very old. A recently-published piece of Mark's Gospel has been dated to somewhere between 150-250 AD.[37] The 'John Rylands Papyrus' is a manuscript fragment that contains part of the Gospel of John, and it is probably from the second century. So, we may trust that God has preserved manuscripts of the New Testament such as these (and many others) for us, and that we therefore have access with unparalleled levels of certainty to what was originally written.

4. Bible Translations

The Bible itself assumes that it will be translated. Every time an Old Testament text is quoted in the New Testament (which happens nearly 700 times), it is quoted in translation. As the events of Pentecost demonstrate, the Word of God is meant to go out to people of all nations, in languages they can understand. So, the Gospel can be preached to the ends of the earth without everyone having to learn Greek and Hebrew—Good News indeed!

As we've seen, Bible translations are not inspired or inerrant. By definition, they are not 'perfect.' But God has commissioned the translation of Scripture. And he is pleased to use translations in the preaching of the Gospel, to save and to strengthen his people. A translation is good to the extent that it is a faithful rendering of the original. There are ongoing debates about 'translation theory,' and each English-language translation reflects a slightly different approach. I'm not going to enter into those debates here. When we choose a Bible translation, most of us have to do so on trust. Not many readers of this book will have enough proficiency in Hebrew or Greek, or all the other different academic disciplines required to produce our own faithful translation of the

Bible. Indeed, few of us have sufficient tools to make an informed judgment about the translations of others. But we *can* ask about the credentials of the translators, or see which translations are trusted and recommended by the leaders in our churches. For example, I would suggest that you avoid the *New World Translation* of the Bible, which is published by the Jehovah's Witnesses. Certain passages in this Bible are translated in such a way as to deny the full divinity of Jesus Christ.

In this book, I've used the English Standard Version (ESV). It's a good translation, and I read it every day. I highly recommend it. But it's not perfect. In mid-2016, the publishers of the ESV (Crossway) announced that the current edition would become the final 'permanent text' edition of the ESV, 'unchanged forever, in perpetuity.' I don't think that was a good idea. If you've followed the argument of this book, perhaps you can see why. Not only do developments in textual criticism continue to suggest changes to the Hebrew, Aramaic and Greek texts of the Bible used by translators, but the English language itself continues to change and evolve. God has

The New World Translation renders John 1:1 like this: 'In the beginning was the Word, and the Word was with God, and the Word was a god.' The inclusion of the indefinite article before the word 'god'— and the small 'g'—suggest that Jesus was not equal in divinity to the Father. This translation is unacceptable, because (a) it is based on a misunderstanding of Greek grammar;[45] (b) it contradicts other statements in Scripture that make clear the equal divinity of the Father and the Son (such as John 5:18); (c) it represents a departure from the Trinitarian faith of the one, holy, catholic, and apostolic church.

not tied himself to the preservation of one particular text, and neither should we. Obviously, enough people agreed with me, because just a month after the original announcement, Crossway reversed its decision, declaring it to have been a 'mistake.'[38]

Translations of Scripture may not be perfect. But God intends the Bible to be translated, and good translations are certainly sufficient for his purposes. We'll be thinking more about those purposes in the next chapter.

Drawing the strands together

You may be in the habit of reading the Bible regularly. If you are, I wonder if you've had the experience of finding that the particular part of Scripture you read on a certain day spoke powerfully to you, almost as though it was meant for you at that time, and in those circumstances? Or perhaps a sermon or talk on a particular passage felt like it was spoken just for you?

This is a common Christian experience. God uses his living Word to speak into our lives. It's true that human beings need '*every* word that comes from the mouth of God' (Matt. 4:4), but we don't necessarily need every word all at once. God, in his sovereignty, speaks to us through those words that are appropriate for us at the right times. This is true, not just for individual believers, but for the church as a whole. As we saw in the last chapter, all God's inspired words are necessary for God's people for all time. But 'for all time' doesn't necessarily mean 'at all times.'

We know that revelation from God was given *progressively*—that is to say, God revealed himself to humanity with ever-increasing clarity over many years. The Bible itself was written down over a period of many centuries. We also know that parts of the Bible could be 'lost' at times. In 2 Chronicles 34:14-21, Hilkiah the priest 'finds' the Book of the Law, during a spring clean at the Temple. We can be sure that God ensured its preservation there, but preservation doesn't imply constant availability, just as translation doesn't imply perfection.

One of the reasons many Christians have preferred the idea that God has preserved his Word in one or more particular manuscripts or translations is that they want to ensure that Scripture has been constantly (and completely) available to the whole church. But neither the Bible itself, nor the nature of God's revelation, demand this sort of availability. God is sovereign over the availability of Scripture at different times and in different places. Sometimes there will be 'a famine [...] of hearing the words of the LORD' (Amos 8:11). But for all time, all of Scripture will be preserved.

We're now in a place to respond to Bart Ehrman's challenge. Remember what Ehrman says: 'How does it help us to say that the Bible is the inerrant Word of God if in fact we don't have the words that God inerrantly inspired, but only the words copied by the scribes—sometimes correctly but sometimes (many times!) incorrectly?' Ehrman is quite right that we don't have direct access to the inspired autographs, or to miraculously-preserved copies. But he is wrong to suggest that we therefore 'don't have' the words that God inspired. As we've seen, God has preserved these words in the canon and manuscript tradition of both testaments, and has decreed that they should be made available to us in translations as well. We do indeed have 'access' to these words, if not with miraculous perfection, then with an extremely high level of accuracy and certainty. And God has done this. What is good enough for the Holy Spirit is good enough for me.

I remember one of my professors in Bible College telling us that God can, in his sovereignty, use a boring sermon, based on a wrong interpretation, of a poor translation, of a bad copy of the Bible. I think that's true. But I wouldn't want to defend that kind of ministry. If the argument presented in this book is correct, God has in his sovereignty given us all the tools we need to equip appropriately-gifted Christians to preach powerful sermons based on a correct interpretation of a Bible translated faithfully from a text that is the same as, or else extremely close to, what was originally written, because God has preserved it for us. In other words, we have *good reason* to trust our sheep-like instincts as we hear his Word.

Now, talk of equipping, gifting and ministry suggests one further question we must explore: *Why* has God preserved Scripture for us?

4

WHY DOES GOD PRESERVE SCRIPTURE?

The LORD will fulfil his purpose for me;
Your steadfast love, O LORD, endures forever.
Do not forsake the work of your hands (Ps. 138:8).

A COMMON (WRONG) ANSWER:
SO THERE'S NOTHING LEFT FOR US TO DO.

I've been to see Lenin's 'preserved' body in Red Square in Moscow. Lenin died in 1924, but his body has been on display in his mausoleum almost ever since. It has to be kept in a special environment, and continuously looked after, at great expense, to prevent further decay. But Lenin is never going to awake from his sleep, at least not until Jesus returns (Daniel 12:2). All that has been preserved is the 'appearance' of life.

When we talk of the 'preservation' of Scripture, we must not allow ourselves to be led astray by ideas of death and decay, or artificially maintaining the appearance of life. The Word of God is not preserved in this sense: it is *living* and *active* (Hebrews 4:12).

The *Westminster Confession of Faith* talks of God's 'singular care and providence' in preserving the Scriptures. Etymologically (and theologically) God is the primary 'curator' of the Bible.[39] As we've seen, this does involve the preservation of real manuscripts, some of which are indeed kept in museums. But again, God is not a 'curator' in the sense of caring for a museum piece, which is now merely to be admired and kept at a distance. It is to be *used*, both by God and by us.

That the Word of God is *alive*, and that it is to be *used*, suggests that in one sense God's work of preservation cannot be considered complete. Scripture has been preserved for a *purpose*. In this chapter, we'll think about that purpose, and the part we have to play in fulfilling it. We can be confident that God has preserved Scripture for us. But too often, evangelical Christians like me have taught a high doctrine of Scripture while failing to live in the light of what that Scripture reveals and teaches. The Bible has stayed in the pocket, or on the shelf, and so questions about the preservation of Scripture have become mere academic curiosities.

In this final chapter, I want us to think about *why* God has preserved Scripture for us. There are two parts to the argument. First, we'll consider why God has preserved a *written* Bible for us (rather than, say, a message to pass

We can truly have God's Word 'in our hands' or even 'in our pockets.' But believing that is one thing: it is not meant to be an end in itself! Equally, it certainly doesn't mean that we somehow 'control' God's Word, or that we've got it 'all wrapped-up.' Twentieth-century 'neo-orthodox' theologian Karl Barth objected to the traditional doctrine of inspiration at least in part because he wanted to avoid this sort of presumptuous attitude towards God's revelation. Even if we disagree with Barth's doctrine of Scripture, as I do, we can register agreement with him that this is an attitude towards the Bible that we must strive to avoid.

on by word-of-mouth alone). Second, we'll think about what *our* responsibility is in relation to the Scripture that has been preserved for us. As we'll see, even when the discussion turns to our responsibilities and response, God is always at work. This chapter is particularly written for Christians. I hope that if you're not a Christian, you will see what a great privilege (and responsibility) has been given to Christians, and that you might catch something of the excitement and the vital urgency of the message and the task with which we've been entrusted.

JAPANESE WHISPERS:
PRESERVED FOR OUR CERTAINTY

I've lived for seven years in Japan, and during that time I learned about its history and culture. For over 200 years, from the 1630s to the 1850s, Japan was almost totally closed off to the outside world. In the previous period, from 1549, Christianity had flourished in parts of the country, and there had been more than 100,000 converts. But in the seventeenth century the Tokugawa Shoguns turned against Christians and began to persecute them.[40]

Christianity became illegal, and Christians were tortured and executed. It was thought that all Christians had disappeared from Japan. In fact, however, a small number kept a version of their faith alive, passing it on mostly by word-of-mouth from generation to generation.

When Japan re-opened its borders in the 1850s, a Roman Catholic priest was astonished to meet a Japanese who told him 'our hearts are as yours.' These people came to be known as the 'hidden Christians.' But, after more than two centuries of secret transmission, the hidden Christians' 'Bible' had become corrupted. It was finally written down in the nineteenth century, but it is clear that things had changed considerably over time. As one historian summarises:

> The first man is called Adan [*sic.*], created on the seventh day along with the first woman, Ewa. Lucifer, another of the creations of Deus [God], demands that Adan and Ewa should worship him. [...] Ewa is swindled into eating the forbidden fruit, and as a result, she and Adan are cursed for 400 million years. The children of Ewa are sentenced to live on the Earth and worship unworthy gods, until a future date when Deus will send a messenger to show them the way back to heaven.

If you're familiar with the early chapters of *Genesis*, some of this will sound vaguely familiar. But when we get to the New Testament, things become even more garbled:

> Mary becomes pregnant by swallowing a butterfly, and spurns the advances of a covetous king in the Philippines. Mary gives birth in a stable, and three days later she is

allowed into the inkeeper's house for a bath. Reusing the bathwater, as is usual in Japan, the inkeeper's son, who suffers from a skin disease, is miraculously cured after touching the same waters as the infant messiah.

The kings of Turkey, Mexico and France come to offer their congratulations on the birth of Jesus (in a stable), but they tell their story to King Herodes, who orders the massacre of all children - his two henchmen are named as Pontia and Pilate. Fleeing to Egypt across the river Baptism, Jesus and Mary are protected by local farmers, whose crops magically grow as soon as they are sown; farmers who refused to help them are stuck with barren fields. The young Jesus argues over matters of religious doctrine with Buddhist priests, before he is betrayed by Judas, executed and then brought back from the dead.[41]

It sounds like quite a tale. The point is that a revelation from God which is *not* committed to writing, and then preserved as a written document, would be liable to get 'lost in transmission,' a bit like Chinese Whispers.[42]

Christians have often observed that God committed the Bible to writing, and then preserved his *written* words, precisely because of the extreme importance of the message. A written message allows for more accurate preservation, more careful study, and greater accessibility.

BEAUTIFUL FEET:
PRESERVED FOR OUR PROCLAMATION

And the LORD answered me: 'Write the vision; make it plain on tablets, so he may run who reads it.' (Hab. 2:2)

As Christians, we have the responsibility to make God's Word known. Scripture has been written down and preserved for us, that we might share it. Take a moment to think about all the things that have happened, over many centuries, in the ordinary providence of God, for the Bible to get to you, right down to the person or people who first shared the Gospel with you. Does that not make you want to give thanks to God?

But God's work doesn't stop with you. He wants you to share Scripture with others. According to *Wycliffe Bible Translators*, the complete Bible has been translated into 670 languages, and a further 1,521 have a New Testament and some portions. There is also known translation and/ or linguistic development happening in 2,584 languages. But there are 7,099 languages known to be in use.[43]

In 1917, a man named William Cameron Townsend went to Guatemala to sell Bibles in Spanish. One day, a Cakchiquel Indian challenged him, 'If your God is so great, why doesn't he speak in my language?' Townsend took up the challenge. He moved to live among the tribe, learned their language and pioneered a writing system in order to translate the Bible. By 1931, the Cakchiquel New Testament was published.[44]

Perhaps someone reading this book will see the needs and the opportunities for the ongoing work of translating the Bible, and consider getting involved. *Wycliffe Bible Translators* would be a good place to start. Someone else may think of the ongoing scholarship needed in textual criticism, and translation into established languages like English, and be led to devote their lives to that work, for the sake of the church. A first port of call would be the relevant books in the resources section at the end of this book.

Not many of us will become vocational Bible translators or scholars. But God still wants every Christian to share the Scripture he has preserved for us. You can do that every time you pass on the Bible's message to others, or chat about what you've been reading in the Bible, or write or tweet Bible verses to your friends. The message of the Bible isn't just good advice for living a happy life. It's the living Word of God, about his Son, inspired by his Holy Spirit. It concerns the deepest issues of eternal importance. Our response to it involves life and death. Sharing this message is both a privilege and a responsibility.

I remember going to one church for the first time as a visiting preacher. A gentleman greeted me, saying, 'Are *you* the one with beautiful feet?' For a moment I thought he must be a bit confused: I certainly was! But then I realised he was referring to Isaiah 52:7. 'How beautiful upon the mountains are the feet of him who brings good news, who publishes peace, who brings good news of happiness, who publishes salvation, who says to Zion, 'Your God reigns.' God has preserved his Word for us. We can run with it. And when we share it, our feet will be counted beautiful by those who receive it in faith.

How might God be calling, preparing, and equipping you to serve him in the ongoing work of preserving his Word?

'CONSUMING' SCRIPTURE:
PRESERVED FOR OUR TRANSFORMATION

In chapter one we looked briefly at 2 Timothy 3:15-16:

> [T]he sacred writings [...] are able to make you wise for
> salvation through faith in Christ Jesus. All Scripture is
> breathed out by God and profitable for teaching, for reproof,
> for correction, and for training in righteousness, that the
> man of God may be competent, equipped for every good
> work.

On the basis of these verses I suggested that God has
given us the Bible for a particular purpose, which I
summarised in chapter one as *enabling the establishment
of fellowship with God*. This involves both our *conversion*
and our *growth*. It follows that we *need* the Bible to live
the Christian life.

The biblical metaphor that best captures this need
is that of the Word of God as *food*. Deuteronomy 8:3
says 'man does not live by bread alone, but man lives by
every word that comes from the mouth of the LORD.'
Put simply, we need to eat to live: just so, for spiritual
life we need the Word of God. God's Word in the Bible
is spiritual food for us, giving us the nourishment to
sustain life. The apostle Peter tells Christians they have
been born again 'through the living and abiding word of
God' (1 Pet. 1:23). Now, Peter commands them, they are
to 'long for the pure spiritual milk' (baby food!) which
surely refers to the same Word of God, 'that by it you

may grow up to salvation' (2:2). This applies also to all of us who are believers today: we are to 'long for' the Word of God, because by it we have been brought to life, and without it we can't continue to live—growing, loving, serving, worshipping, and glorifying God—as we were created to do.

In chapter two we read about a king, Jehoiakim, who burned Scripture. But there are other ways to 'consume' Scripture, without it being consumed by flames. More than once in the Bible we read about people who, literally, *ate* Scripture (or at least books with God-given words on them). The prophet Ezekiel was told: 'feed your belly with this scroll that I give you and fill your stomach with it' (Ezekiel 3:3). Likewise the Apostle John was commanded to eat a scroll from the hand of an angel (Revelation 10:9). Both men apparently enjoyed the experience, as the scrolls turned out to be as 'sweet as honey' in their mouths. (John does seem to have got an upset tummy, though!) Fortunately, God's purposes for us don't require us to eat the Bible *physically*. We've to eat *spiritually*.

Much of the time, our Bible-reading and Bible-hearing (gathered together with God's people) may not

What place does the Bible have in our lives? I don't mean theoretically, or doctrinally. I'm not asking now what we believe about the Bible. I'm asking what we do with the Bible. Are we feeding daily on God's Word? When God's Word is read and preached to us, are we ready for God to give us a feast?

feel particularly 'spiritual.' Daily Bible-reading can be hard work, and it involves us engaging our minds as well as our hearts. But it's spiritual because the Holy Spirit is at work when we read. We've no grounds for separating 'Word' and 'Spirit' in the Christian life, because the Bible is the Spirit's. He is the one who uses God's words to achieve God's purposes for us as we read in faith, ready for God to transform us. Theologians say that the Spirit *illuminates* (gives light) as we read. That's the climax of the process that began when the Spirit inspired (or 'breathed out') the words of Scripture. Just as he inspired the words, so he preserved them. And just as he preserved the words of Scripture for us, so he takes them and applies them to our hearts and minds, so that we are reconciled to the Father through faith in Jesus, and he begins to work in us as we work out our salvation. As he does so, not one of his good promises fails (Joshua 21:45).

For just these purposes, then, God's Word is preserved *for us*: for our certainty, for our proclamation, and for our transformation. Scripture isn't preserved like a museum-piece or an embalmed body is 'preserved.' That's because the Word of God isn't dead: it's *living and active*. As we've seen, some of these divine purposes for the Bible and for believers entail great responsibilities and privileges for us. But through it all *God* is the one who works, in and through his Word, and in and through us, for the sake of the world. His steadfast love endures forever. He will not forsake the work of his hands.

CONCLUSION

> For whatever was written in former days was written for
> our instruction, that through endurance and through the
> encouragement of the Scriptures we might have hope. May
> the God of endurance and encouragement grant you to live
> in such harmony with one another, in accord with Christ
> Jesus (Rom. 15:4–5).

We've covered quite a bit of ground in a few short pages.
We've seen that the God of Scripture has preserved
Scripture, by his marvellous providence, through the work
of countless 'ordinary' men and women, with glorious
purposes in mind. I hope this book has encouraged you
to love God and his Word more, and perhaps cleared up
some questions you or your friends have wondered about.

I've talked a lot about what God does in this book. I
think it's good to be reminded that our God is alive, and
working, and speaking, *always*. Preserving the Bible for
us is just one of those works. Because God has preserved
his Word in Scripture, we can be sure that *when Scripture*

speaks, God speaks. Because God has preserved Scripture for us, we can have every confidence that we are hearing his voice in Scripture.

Did you notice, in the verses from Romans 15 above, the connection between God, on the one hand, and Scripture, on the other? If you're anything like me as a reader, you probably skipped over those Bible verses, so have a closer look. According to the first sentence, which is verse 4, the Scriptures (Paul, who wrote Romans, means the Old Testament Scriptures here) give us *endurance* and *encouragement*. But the Scriptures don't do this because they have some kind of magical properties. As the second sentence (verse 5) makes clear, *God* is the one who is the true source of *endurance* and *encouragement*. When Scripture *instructs* us, it is really God himself who is instructing us and giving us hope. These verses always remind me of the extremely close connection between God and his written Word. When Scripture speaks, God himself speaks.

It's clear to me that such an equation demands a doctrine of the preservation of Scripture. Indeed, Paul seems to assume as much when he writes that 'whatever was written in former days' is still available to the Christians of his day, whether in Rome or elsewhere. So I could have included these verses back in chapter one. But I wanted to save them for this conclusion because of the powerful way in which they underline *God's* ongoing work in and through Scripture.

Some Christians end their Bible readings in church services with the words, 'This is the Word of the Lord.'

And the congregation responds: 'Thanks be to God!' Whether we say those words or not, the point is right and true. God speaks *today* as his ancient words are read. So, next time you're going to read the Bible, I hope you'll do so with renewed confidence that God will indeed speak to you, feed you, and work in you, by the words that he has preserved, according to his glorious purposes for you. *Thanks be to God!*

SUGGESTIONS FOR FURTHER READING

If you would like to read more, or consider further some of the issues touched on in this book, there are many excellent resources that cover various aspects of the doctrine of Scripture from an evangelical perspective. The best recent books include:

Feinberg, John S. *Light in a Dark Place: The Doctrine of Scripture*. Wheaton: Crossway, 2018.

Feinberg's book is very thorough, and particularly strong on the inerrancy of Scripture. Unusually for works of this kind, he includes a chapter on preservation. Most of his conclusions are similar to mine, although he prefers to say that it is 'highly probable' that God should preserve Scripture rather than logically 'necessary.' Even so, he writes, 'the probability is so high that while it is imaginable [...] that God would not preserve his Word, it is so likely that he would, that it makes little sense to doubt that he would.' (p. 750)

Frame, John. *A Theology of Lordship*. vol. 4. *The Doctrine of the Word of God*. Phillipsburg: P & R Publishing, 2010.

Frame's work is extremely useful. Highlights of this book include a chapter on 'Bible problems' and the introductory chapters on the doctrine of revelation.

Ward, Timothy. *Words of Life: Scripture as the Living and Active Word of God*. Leicester: IVP, 2009.

Ward's book is a much shorter read (less than a third of the length of either Frame or Feinberg) but still very helpful. A particular strength of this book is its Trinitarian approach to the doctrine of Scripture.

If you are interested in textual criticism and the story of 'how we got the Bible' in particular, you might want to try these introductory texts:

Lanier, Gregory R. *A Christian's Pocket Guide to How We Got the Bible*. Fearn: Christian Focus, 2018.

Brotzman, Ellis R. *Old Testament Textual Criticism: A Practical Introduction*. Grand Rapids: Baker, 1994.

Metzger, Bruce M. and Bart D. Ehrman. *The Text of the New Testament: Its Transmission, Corruption, and Restoration*. 4th ed. Oxford: Oxford University Press, 2005.

Readers may be surprised to see a book by Ehrman recommended here. I do not endorse all Ehrman's conclusions, certainly in many of his other books, but this book is a readable and sensible introduction to the issues.

ENDNOTES

1   For example, one recent and extensive, evangelical collection of essays on the question of Scripture's authority, edited by D. A. Carson (*The Enduring Authority of the Christian Scriptures* [Grand Rapids: Eerdmans, 2016]), contains only two references to providence. Both of these are found in the chapter by Graham A. Cole, 'Why a Book? Why This Book? Why the Particular Order within This Book? Some Theological Reflections on the Canon,' 456-476. Cole argues that the doctrine of Scripture as a whole 'may usefully be located within the doctrine of special providence' (466n28), and that 'divine providence [was] at work in the formation of the canon' (468).

2   Compare the gloss in the *Oxford English Dictionary*: 'conforming exactly with the truth or with a given standard; free from error' (*s.v.* accurate).

3   We don't know for sure what writing materials were originally used for the biblical books. For the OT, leather seems most likely. For the NT, papyrus is the strongest candidate.

4   Qur'ān scholar Keith E. Small, in his book *Textual Criticism and Qur'ān Manuscripts* (Lexington Books: Minneapolis, 2011) has demonstrated this point in respect of the text of the Qur'ān. His conclusion is that 'the history of the transmission of the text of the Qur'ān is at least as much a testament to the *destruction* of Qur'ān material as it is to its *preservation*.' Ibid., 180, emphasis mine.

5 Dan Brown, *The Da Vinci Code* (New York: Doubleday, 2003).

6 Bart D. Ehrman, *The Orthodox Corruption of Scripture: The Effect of Early Christological Controversies on the Text of the New Testament* (Oxford: Oxford University Press, 2011), xi.

7 For a more detailed discussion of the issues raised by textual criticism see Lanier, *How We Got the Bible.*

8 See the essay by Daniel B. Wallace, 'Inspiration, Preservation, and New Testament Textual Criticism,' in *New Testament Essays in Honor of Homer A. Kent, Jr,* ed. Gary T. Meadors (Winona Lake: BMH Books, 1991).

9 Note that I am not drawing a distinction here between the words of Scripture, and its underlying message, as though the actual words are in some sense secondary to the meaning. The message of the Bible is fundamentally dependent on its words, phrases, and sentences.

10 Chapter 1.6 of the *Westminster Confession of Faith* says, 'The whole counsel of God, concerning all things necessary for His own glory, man's salvation, faith and life, is either expressly set down in Scripture, or by good and necessary consequence may be deduced from Scripture: unto which nothing at any time is to be added, whether by new revelations of the Spirit, or traditions of men.'

For an excellent summary of what this statement means for doctrinal formulation see the chapter, 'Interpreting the Bible: The Text and its Implications,' in the volume in this series by Robert Letham, *A Christian's Pocket Guide to Baptism* (Fearn: Christian Focus, 2012), 5-8.

11 The word 'preservation' is not used: the confession speaks of Scripture being 'kept.' The Latin version has '*custodita*,' which gives us our English word 'custodian.' Again, the sense is of 'taking care' of Scripture.

12 Robert Letham, in his analysis of the Westminster Assembly's theology, says that the confession's assertion that the Hebrew text of the Old Testament and the Greek text of the New Testament were 'immediately inspired by God' is 'an appeal to the original *autographa*.' (Robert Letham, *The Westminster Assembly: Reading Its Theology in Historical Context* [Phillipsburg: P&R Pub, 2009], 144.)

Since inspiration, rightly understood, applies only to the act of the

Spirit in this initial writing of the Bible, this is self-evidently the case, but we should not therefore conclude that the Assembly declared the *autographa* alone to be the 'authentical' scriptures.

In a book published in the same year as the *Westminster Confession of Faith* (1647), Edward Leigh—who was a member of the Westminster Assembly—wrote that, 'The Hebrew of the old Testament and the Greeke of the new is the authentique Edition, and the pure fountain of divine truth.' Leigh clarified his position as follows: 'When we speake of the originall and authenticke Text of Holy Scripture, that is not to be so understood as if we meant it of the Autographs written by the hand of Moses, or the other Prophets or Apostles, but onely of the originall or the primogeniall Text in that tongue, out of which divers versions were derived according to the variety of tongues.' (Edward Leigh, *A Treatise of Divinity* [London: Printed by E. Griffin for William Lee, 1647], 101-102.)

For more on this point, see my article, '*Ad Fontes!*—The Concept of the "Originals" of Scripture in Seventeenth-Century Reformed Orthodoxy,' in *Westminster Theological Journal*, Spring 2019, Vol. 81 Issue 1, 123-139.

13   For example, John Owen argued for the providential preservation of Scripture on the basis of the 'constant consent of all copies in the world.' See John Owen, *Of the Divine Original, Authority, Self-evidencing Light, and Power of the Scriptures*, in *The Works of John Owen*, ed. William H. Goold, (Edinburgh: Johnstone and Hunter, 1853), vol. XVI, 358, reprinted by The Banner of Truth Trust, 1968.

14   See, for example, the *Chicago Statement on Biblical Inerrancy*, available online at http://www.bible-researcher.com/chicago1.html (accessed 27 September 2018).

15   The *Westminster Confession of Faith* (5.1) speaks of God's 'most wise and holy providence' as the means by which God 'direct[s], dispose[s], and govern[s] all creatures, actions, and things, from the greatest even to the least, [...] according to His infallible foreknowledge, and the free and immutable counsel of His own will, to the praise of the glory of His wisdom, power, justice, goodness, and mercy.'

16   John Webster, 'Providence,' in Michael Allen and Scott R.

Swain (eds.) *Christian Dogmatics: Reformed Theology for the Church Catholic* (Grand Rapids: Baker, 2016), 150.

17　Ibid., 157.

18　See allusions to the story in Irenaeus, *Against Heresies*, Book III, 21.2; Clement of Alexandria, *Stromata*, Book I, 22; Tertullian, *De Cultu Feminarum*, Book I, 3.2.

19　The legend was based on a text called the *Letter of Aristeas*, which purported to be a contemporary account of the translation of the Old Testament into Greek. An account of the *Letter*'s history and reception may be found in Abraham Wasserstein and David J. Wasserstein, *The Legend of the Septuagint: From Classical Antiquity to Today* (Cambridge: Cambridge University Press, 2009).

Wasserstein and Wasserstein conclude—in unanimity with almost all scholarship from the seventeenth century onwards—that the *Letter* was a 'pseudepigraphon, that is that the author was not the man he pretended to be' (22). The *Letter* contains 'an important element of pretence,' and 'at least some of the details of this narrative are pure invention that could not possibly have been true' (23). Yet some, like Archbishop Ussher (1581-1656), defended the *Letter* as a reliable source, without necessarily accepting all details of the 'legend' that grew up around it.

20　Puritan theologian John Owen defines 'miracles' as 'such effects as are really beyond and above the power of natural causes, however applied unto operation.' These were, he writes, 'all the immediate effects of the divine power of the Holy Ghost.'

See John Owen, *Pneumatologia: Or, A Discourse Concerning the Holy Spirit*, in *The Works of John Owen*, vol. 3 (Edinburgh: Banner of Truth, 1965), 145.

21　Deism is belief in the existence of a supreme being, specifically of a creator who does not intervene in the universe.

22　See Simon Keynes, 'The Reconstruction of a Burnt Cottonian Manuscript: The Case of Cotton MS. Otho. A.1,' in *The British Library Journal*, vol. 22, no. 2 (Autumn 1996), 113-160. I'm grateful to Elijah Hixson for drawing my attention to this story.

23　John Calvin, *Institutes*, Book I.viii.10.

24   The declaration of the (Roman Catholic) Council of Trent (1546) that the Latin Vulgate alone was authentic Scripture was followed by the publication of standard editions of the Vulgate in 1590 (the Sixtine Vulgate) and 1592 (the Clementine Vulgate).

25   As we've noted above, in the discussion of the letter *yodh*, the *autograph* of Genesis would have been written in different characters (palaeo-Hebrew script). But the basic point I'm making here still stands.

26   For example, Lewis Capellus (1585-1658), a learned French Protestant and Professor of Hebrew at Saumur, published (anonymously) his *Arcanum Punctationis Revelatum: The Mystery of the Punctuation Revealed* in 1624. His later book of proposed emendations to the text of the Old Testament, *Critica Sacra*, carried the subtitle: 'in which the many different readings observed in places of Holy Scripture are explicated, illustrated, and not a few thus emended.' Richard Muller explains the effect of Capellus' work on his own Protestant constituency: 'It seemed as if the the textual underpinnings of the Reformation's *sola scriptura* were being chipped away from within the ranks of the Reformed.' See Richard A. Muller, 'The Debate Over the Vowel Points and the Crisis in Orthodox Hermeneutics,' in *After Calvin: Studies in the Development of a Theological Tradition* (Oxford: Oxford University Press, 2003), 149.

27   See https://news.byu.edu/news/byu-professor-named-editor-new-edition-hebrew-old-testament, accessed 28 September 2018.

28   The material in this chapter has some overlap with Lanier, *How We Got the Bible*, where points relating to textual criticism and canon are treated in greater detail.

29   See Lanier, *How We Got the Bible*, especially chapters 2 and 4.

30   Meredith G. Kline, *The Structure of Biblical Authority*, 2nd ed. (Eugene: Wipf and Stock, 1997).

31   Ellis R. Brotzman, *Old Testament Textual Criticism: A Practical Introduction* (Grand Rapids: Baker, 1994).

32   A line from the hymn, *Amazing Grace*, by John Newton.

33   This example is found in Bruce M. Metzger and Bart D. Ehrman, *The Text of the New Testament: Its Transmission, Corruption,*

and Restoration, 4ᵗʰ ed. (Oxford: Oxford University Press, 2005), 259.

34 Peter J. Gurry, 'The Number of Variants in the Greek New Testament: A Proposed Estimate,' in *New Testament Studies*, vol. 62, no. 1 (January 2016), 97-121 at 113.

35 Gurry, 'The Number of Variants,' 97.

36 Daniel B. Wallace, *Revisiting the Corruption of the New Testament: Manuscript, Patristic, and Apocryphal Evidence* (Grand Rapids: Kregel Publications, 2011), 43. By 'viable,' Wallace means a variant 'found in manuscripts with a sufficient pedigree that they have some likelihood of reflecting the original wording.' By 'meaningful,' he means that 'the variant changes the meaning of the text *to some degree*.' (Ibid., 40, 42.)

37 See the article of 30 May 2018 by Elijah Hixson at https://www.christianitytoday.com/ct/2018/may-web-only/mark-manuscript-earliest-not-first-century-fcm.html (accessed 27 September 2018).

38 See 'Crossway Statement on the ESV Bible Text,' https://www.crossway.org/articles/crossway-statement-on-the-esv-bible-text/ (accessed 27 September 2018).

39 From the Latin *cura* (='care'). Readers may recall from the introduction that 'accurate' has a similar etymology. An 'accurate' Bible is one that has been 'taken care of' (by God).

40 This period of persecution was the subject of the 2016 Hollywood film, *Silence*, directed by Martin Scorsese.

41 Jonathan Clements, *Christ's Samurai: The True Story of the Shimabara Rebellion* (London: Robinson, 2016), 209-210.

42 This game is known as 'telephone' in the USA.

43 https://www.wycliffe.org.uk/about/faq/.

44 This story is found in James B. Williams and Randolph Shaylor (eds.), *God's Word in Our Hands: The Bible Preserved for Us* (Greenville: Ambassador, 2003), 285.

45 On this point, see Daniel B. Wallace, *Greek Grammar Beyond the Basics: An Exegetical Syntax of the New Testament* (Grand Rapids: Zondervan, 1996), 266-269.